> "It is very certain that, as to all persons who have killed themselves, the Devil put the cord round their necks. . ."
>
> MARTIN LUTHER

Also by Mary Savage

TENDERLY, MY LOVE (1960), novel
JUST FOR TONIGHT (1961), novel
A LIKENESS TO VOICES (1963), novel
THE COACH DRAWS NEAR (1964), novel
SAVORY STEWS (1969), cookbook

ADDICTED TO SUICIDE

a woman
struggling
to live

MARY SAVAGE

SCHENKMAN PUBLISHING COMPANY
Cambridge, Massachusetts

New edition © 1979
Schenkman Publishing Company
3 Mt. Auburn Place
Cambridge, MA 02138

First published by
Capra Press, Santa Barbara
California in 1975.
Copyright © 1975 by Mary Savage

Library of Congress Cataloging in Publication Data

Savage, Mary.
  Addicted to suicide.
  Reprint, with new foreword and afterword, of the 1975
ed. published by Capra Press, Santa Barbara, Calif.
  1. Savage, Mary—Biography. 2. Mental illness—
Biography. 3. Authors, English—20th century—Biography.
I. Title.
PS3569.A828Z463 1979   362.2′092′4 [B]   79-4695
ISBN 0-87073-906-9
ISBN 0-87073-907-7 pbk.

Printed in the United States of America.

All rights reserved. This book, or parts thereof,
may not be reproduced in any form without written
permission of the publisher.

FOREWORD

WHEN I ORIGINALLY wrote the second part of this book, I was in a state of euphoria. I was filled with confidence and vitality, touched by the presence of God in my life. I tried to convey something of that feeling and the experiences surrounding it, but my efforts fell far short of success. I knew from reactions to the book, which was published four years ago, that the central message of recovery from depression had been lost in the details of the depression itself.

I wrote of salvation as if it were a one-time event, a single bolt of lightning that transformed my life from what it was into something else—for now and all time hereafter. I wrote of myself as having crossed the street to the sunny side and I expected to remain there, untroubled, capable, blessed. But a lightning flash illumines for only a few seconds and then the world returns to its previous condition. My glimpse of transcendence dissolved in the reality of day-to-day living. True, I had gathered up my fragments and was a whole—if not new—person. But clouds gathered across the sun because salvation, in order to be permanent, must be recurrent. Conversion does not last unless one repeats one's vows.

A question most frequently asked was, "How did you manage to shake off your addiction? What cured you?" When I wrote the book, I didn't really know. It seemed that a miracle had taken place while I was down with pneumonia in the hospital, a miracle which brought about a change in direction. Today, I can only answer the questions by saying that I worked at it. Because of my illness, because of all the therapy, because of the love of my husband and son, I saw that suicide was no longer an alternative. I cannot attribute my "cure" to any one thing, nor can I say to others, "This is how you go about it." I cannot do this because life is not that simple—there are no easy, or easily-applied answers to the problems life poses. Life is a process, a continual shifting and changing of values, ideas, and perceptions. One must constantly synthesize new resolutions.

When the suggestion was first made to me that this book should be kept in print, I was tempted to sit down and rewrite the whole book, adding and deleting from the vantage point of the elapsed four years. Then I realized that the value of the book lay in its immediacy. It was written as I was experiencing the feelings and events it describes. In that sense, it should remain as it was written, with only an Afterword to bring it up to date.

Now, as then, I offer it to those who wish to understand. As a document, its primary value is honesty. The suicidal state of mind is not a pretty place to visit. Yet, at the end of the book, I wrote, "Thus am I truly come home." And it was true. Despite the trials, both inner and outer, which I have endured since those words were written, I can say that I remained at home in myself. Not always comfortably and not always securely, but with the knowledge that my center was intact.

Depression is a common illness today and there is a growing number of professionals specializing in the study of suicide. With the new edition of this book I hope to add to the body of knowledge concerning the mental condition which leads to attempted suicide, both as an immediate crisis and as a long-term character development. Suicides nearly always telegraph their intentions, yet statistically the highest risk group for successful suicide is among those who have tried it before. (The second highest risk group is alcoholics.) Attempted suicide does become an addiction, a desperate means of coping with unbearable pressures and apparently irremediable pain. I was such an addict, and my story reveals what it feels like to be the victim of that destructive suicidal mind-set. I have written it for those who are students of the affliction as well as for those whose lives have been touched by it.

Mary Savage
January, 1979

PREFACE

THIS BOOK is about an event that didn't quite take place: my own suicide. Over and over I tried to kill myself, specific acts accompanied by the mounting use of alcohol. The desire for death ran through my life like a deep sub-current, mostly invisible but powerfully present. Now and again it surfaced, triggered by some circumstance or some phase of mental illness. In the beginning, these surfacings were relatively harmless, gestures of despair, faint ringings of the alarm bell. But, as time went by, they became increasingly dangerous. The current gathered into itself the greater part of the river. Self-murder preoccupied my mind.

The trend culminated in the events described in this book. One event, perhaps. A coming-together of many forces into a single, central act. That act is the focus of this book, which was written in two parts: before and after.

The first part is a record of my despair, and at the same time an attempt to exorcise it. I had been severely depressed, in the clinical sense, for some time, and I was trying to write my way out of it. At the same time, I was making plans to get out of it in other ways: stockpiling potentially lethal pills, hiding a razor blade, considering when and how to use these weapons. There were two currents, moving side by side, but in opposite directions.

The second part of the book was written some seven or eight months later and views all of this confusion from the other end of the telescope. It is a record of synthesis, of assembly. Where there was chaos, there is now a pattern. Where there were fragments, there is now a person. The sub-current was not eliminated, it was absorbed and re-routed.

Something happened in that interim, and I have written everything I know about it. Why? Not because I know everything there is to know about it—I don't. And not because I think I have found The Answer and am giving it to the world to wear regardless of how it fits—for I don't think there is any one answer; each of us must find his or her own.

I have written about what happened to me because it sheds some light on the processes of mental illness and of suicidal thinking, and we need a lot more light in that still dimly-illuminated room. More important, however, is my hope that somewhere, somehow, my story will give that extra measure of courage to some person struggling in the awful waters of despair. I don't know exactly what made my recovery possible. There were many factors, not the least of which was time. But my message is not in the realm of how or why, it is in the realm of what. This is the way it was; this is the way it is. If it happened to me, it can happen to others.

This deeply personal chronicle was written partly in agony, partly in faith. At its center is a crisis. I would dedicate the book to those who tried to help me before the crisis and to those who did help me afterwards. For the most part, they are the same people, but I make a distinction because, during my illness, I refused to acknowledge their presence or accept their help. My narrowed universe did not include love.

It does now, and I can say Thank you to the people who were willing to make a commitment to my life, thereby ultimately making it possible for me to make a commitment to it.

Mary Savage
April, 1975

PART I
Until April 1974

"The moment I am born, I am old enough to die."
—James Hillman, *Suicide and the Soul.*

THE wheel of my years has spun 48 times and during that period I have tried to destroy myself with pills, with gas, with razor blades, with carbon monoxide and with alcohol. You'll note that I haven't tried drowning or poison or hanging. That's because death, to me, must be painless, like sleep. It isn't that I am afraid. People tell me I should be, but I find no fear of death in me. It is rather that I want the embrace of oblivion to be soft and noiseless, undramatic. I would like to leave this world causing even less of a ripple than I made when I came into it. If I could, I would take an eraser and simply erase myself, my existence, my history, my whole being, and let the waters close over the place where I have been as if it had never existed.

I can't say at what point in my life my obsession with death began. I was an only child until I was nine years old, and with the arrival of my brother, my life was thrown completely out of focus. Fear death? I did indeed. Rings around the moon foretold iminent destruction; a minor kidney ailment I developed at that time would surely be fatal; a broken arm might easily have been a broken neck. I did not hate my brother, because hatred was not allowed and I was above all an obedient child. I am still an obedient child. If a barrier is set around me, I find a way to sidestep it, climb over it, melt through it or outwit it with every appearance of obedience and with, I am told, the "sweetest of smiles." Maybe that has something to do with my obsession with suicide. It is forbidden. Therefore, I must explore it. And when my brother was a baby, I slapped him when nobody was within earshot.

The gap of nine years between my birth when my mother was eighteen and the birth of my brother when she was twenty-seven was neither planned nor accidental. Having given birth to one child, Mother apparently decided she did not wish to repeat the experience. (I suspect that she, too, tried to outmaneuver obstacles with the "sweetest of smiles.") At any rate, she defeated succeeding pregnancies with every then known method of home-abortion of the do-it-yourself variety, including such ingenious devices as clothes hangers, lye douches, and similar tactics, which usually landed her in the hospital. Nevertheless, my brother weighed in at well over nine pounds and grew to be 6'3" tall, which says something about his determination to put in an appearance in this world. I have some thoughts as to whether one's conception and birth may not be acts of will rather than accidents, but that is the subject of another book. This book is about how to get *out* of this world, not *into* it.

Seventeen years after the surprise of my arrival (and I really was a surprise because my mother's mother did not believe in any form of sex education), a second girl outwitted all of Mother's fetus-discouragers, and I had a sister. As my death wish was pretty well established by that time, my sister's arrival did not disturb me. Or perhaps it did, for I made my first suicide attempt at the age of eighteen.

What and how children learn is the subject of much discussion these days, as anyone who has struggled through Piaget and his colleagues can attest. What I learned from Mother's practices was that pregnancy was to be avoided at all costs. In fact, I must have learned it so well that it disappeared into my unconscious where it successfully prevented my conceiving a child. Although I was married twice and had a number of love affairs in between, I did not become pregnant until I reached the age of 39, despite the fact that I never used contraceptives of any kind.

My childhood was spent in a series of small towns, in a series of small schools, in a series of small and mostly unpleasant experiences, out of which I have never been able to make an integrated whole. From the age of twelve, there was greater stability in my physical environment, but I still feel my life has been episodic, and one of my present struggles is to bring some degree of coherence into it. I have described it as an archipelago, a rather aimless string of islands with no obvious connection. I lived for a while in one place doing one thing, and then I jumped to another place doing another thing, but there was no relationship between the two places, no means of communication, no sense of continuity, not even any luggage.

<u>Now I feel the time has come for me to move to another island, but I can't. Too many hands are holding on to me, too many people need me, and I am stifled. I have lost love, and the harder I search for it, the darker everything gets.</u>

I am racked by a fever of the bones. I put out my hand and touch nothing. The earth presses against my chest, but I can see the stars; I am traversing the hardest of passages. Am I alive, or is this death? If I am alive, why am I so alone? If this is death, how do I perceive all of the segments of my knowing as real? The books, the rugs, the pictures, the doors are all as they should be, or have been, or might have been. And the people—they smile, hold hands, dance and cry, but are they as they should be, or have been, or might have been? Are they there at all? Am I? If I could find the thread that binds my life into a whole, then I would know. But in the meantime, this is neither life nor death—it is madness.

My insane self rattles through this body, trying to find a way out. But where did my insanity start? Or was I born with it? The pre-school me lived in a duplex apartment in a fair-sized town in Colorado, where my father worked as a policeman, my mother worked in a laundry, and I was in the care of my crazy grandmother who sat all day with her feet in the oven and did not speak to anyone for months. Our nearest neighbors were my god-parents who, as this was during Prohibition, made home brew and fed a great deal of it to me. At the age of three, I was frequently staggering when my mother came home from work, which may account for my present devotion to fermented beverages. The god-parents had a daughter who, it was whispered when I wasn't supposed to be listening, had to be put in an institution because of her inability to cope with life. A dark and shameful secret, and a good reason for imbibing all that home brew.

We were Lithuanian Catholics and most of our neighbors were Jews; my relationships with the neighborhood children were affected from day to day by their feelings about "goys." On Sundays, I roamed the area begging breakfast, often coming home with my hands full of oranges and cookies. When we had visitors, I was warned by my mother not to reveal that the bites covering my face and arms were caused by bedbugs. We had our dark and shameful secrets, too.

Are these the ingredients of insanity? When I was five, my father went to work for a construction crew of the telephone company, and therewith began the movings from town to town and school to school. Until I was twelve, we moved every three or four months, and I never attended the same school twice. In each new community, the routine was always the same: "What's your name?" "Mary W——." "Mary *what?*" "Mary W——." "How'dya spell it?" "W——." "What kinda name is that? "Lithuanian." "Lithu-what? Where's that?" Finally I started calling myself a Russian because everybody knew where Russia was.

"What's your father do?" they would ask. "He's a mechanic," I would reply. Actually, he was a truck driver, but that was too low on the social scale to be admitted. As it was, the fact that we were so transient made me too much of a peculiar object. The final query was always, "What church d'ya go to?" Instinctively, I avoided answering that one until I had identified the most popular church in town, which then became the church of my choice. As a result, my religious education includes nearly every variety of Christianity extant, including the Pillar of Fire.

Theoretically, all of this should have made me tough. And maybe it did, but I have covered it up with a retiring manner and that sweet smile, for to enter a new community with a tough exterior was asking for trouble. I had trouble enough with my name, my nationality, and my newness.

Give the wheel another spin and see what comes up on the opposite side. Instead of an obsession with death, there is the fear of death. Now that is much more manageable; it is historical, it is universal. It begins in childhood with: Grandpa died. Will you die? Will I? And we get to: "Now I lay me down to sleep, I pray the lord my soul to keep." And we get to angels who watch over you. And we get to death as a form of helplessness, and thence to insomnia because sleep is a form of helplessness and therefore a form of death.

All my adult life, I have struggled with the basic contradiction between insomnia, representing a fear of death on the one hand, and an obsession with death represented by a desire to commit suicide on the other.

Sleep I pursued night after night past the horrendous demons and devils and other dreadful creatures that inhabited the corners of my dark bedroom as a child. Sleep I pursued when I was first a student in college and knew there were no monsters in my bedroom and was all the more terrified for knowing that. Sleep I despaired of when I lived alone in New York City and could not let go of wakefulness until daybreak. So night was my enemy and death was my friend, and never the twain shall meet?

Now I have pills to help me sleep.

When I was eighteen, I took myself off to the state university where I registered as a pre-med student (God bless the illusions of the young). In a fairly short time, I found myself less and less able to concentrate, to sleep, to eat, to converse, to think, or to function at all. I spent most of my free time in a nearby cemetery where it was peaceful and green and the residents were indifferent. I wrote poetry and tore it into shreds and watched it float away on a small stream that wandered among the graves. I envied the dead their tranquillity.

In those days, school dormitories had rules, and one of them was that the girls had to be in their rooms by 10:00 p.m. I ignored that rule one night (sweetly, no doubt), and walked to the home of the school psychologist (by way of the cemetery), where I wrapped myself in some burlap bags in his garage and went to sleep. How it was that I could sleep in these circumstances and not in a warm, comfortable bed, I don't know. At any rate, this kindly gentleman found me in the morning, returned me to my dorm and somehow convinced the Dean of Women that I should not be expelled. I completed the term with an unremarkable academic record.

I understand that the reason for all this internal turmoil was a kind of separation anxiety. It was the first time I had been away from home, and I was very dependent on my parents, especially my mother. And yet, on school holidays, I refused to visit them, but stayed with friends instead. Are all psychological truths represented by contradictions?

When the school term ended, I returned to my home town, but not to my home. I stayed with the mother and stepfather of my best friend, got a job, and once a week visited a psychiatrist. I remember him very clearly as a large man with skin problems. His face was always dotted with little spots of white cream, and as he had a florid complexion, this gave him a clownish appearance. He had a glass-topped desk and when I talked to him, I ran my fingers along the edge of the glass. He told me he was going to unwrap me like an onion. I told him I couldn't sleep. He prescribed phenobarbital. It didn't help. After a month, I went for a walk one night, picked some flowers, scattered them on the lawn, returned to my room and swallowed all the phenobarbital in the box. And slept.

Somewhere around 11:00 the following morning, the firm for which I worked telephoned to inquire about my absence. Dave, my girl friend's stepfather (whom I had known since I was 12), woke me, fed me black coffee, walked me around the house, telephoned my doctor, took me to the county psychiatric hospital and signed me in as a patient. If he had known then how often he was to send me to a hospital when I tried to commit suicide, perhaps he would not have been so compassionate.

I was hospitalized for nearly three months, during which time I was given insulin shock treatments six times a week for six weeks.

Insulin shock is no longer used in the treatment of mental illness as it has been found to be less effective and more dangerous than other methods. A sufficient amount of insulin was injected intravenously to cause unconsciousness and convulsions. Several hours later, the patient awoke to find himself in a bed soaked with perspiration, frequently tied down to the mattress with twisted bedsheets. It was not a pleasant experience. Sometimes I woke up earlier than the other patients and heard them moaning and screaming. Everything was white and damp and surreal; I could not believe this was happening to me.

Care had to be taken that the full effect of the insulin was felt at the time of its administration; a delayed reaction could cause trouble, as any diabetic can tell you. On one occasion, my insulin injection didn't "take" because I was excited about going home for the week-end. (By this time, I had resolved my feelings of repugnance toward my parents.) I was unconscious, but I did not have convulsions, which apparently nobody noticed. Then, as now, hospitals were understaffed.

Later that day, as I was being driven home by my father's

cousin, I went into a coma, which he assumed was normal sleep. We lived some twenty miles from the hospital, and by the time we got home, I was beginning to convulse. Terrified, my mother called the hospital authorities, who told her to try to feed me strong sugar water and to get me back to the hospital as quickly as possible. As my teeth were tightly clenched, she could not administer the sugar water, and my father raced me back to the hospital, with his hand on the horn. When I recovered consciousness, I found myself in a strait-jacket in a padded cell, with a tube running down one nostril carrying a glucose solution into my stomach.

Recalling this incident fills me with sadness. I am struck by the fact that neither of my parents came to the hospital to pick me up for my first visit home after so many months and so much turbulence. I suppose there was a reason for this, but I don't know what is was. I thoroughly disliked the man they sent; he was usually drunk and dirty, and I was uncomfortable in his presence. I can remember now my excitement at the prospect of going home, and my disappointment when this man arrived to take me there.

Life in a mental hospital in 1944 was considerably different than it is in the more liberalized institutions of today. Group therapy had not yet been invented (or was it discovered, like plutonium?), but occupational therapy was a daily part of our routine (I embroidered pillow cases), as was physical therapy, consisting of a supervised walk around the hospital grounds two or three times a week. The psychiatric unit was housed in a separate building from the main hospital. On the ground floor were the administrative offices; on the second floor was the men's ward, and on the third, the women's. Each ward had a special wing reserved for disturbed patients, i.e., those who had to be restrained. The windows of the second and third floors were barred, and all the doors, of which there were a great many, were locked. After every meal, the silverware was counted before the patients were allowed to leave the dining room.

I did, and still do, suffer from vascular headaches, for which no medication was given. Sleeplessness was similarly regarded as unimportant, but after much complaining I was finally given a dose of paraldehyde, after which I decided I would rather stay awake. On the other hand, huge quantities of medication were provided after every meal, half a jigger full of pills and capsules of varying shapes, sizes and colors. I never knew what they were for, and sometimes I wonder if the hospital staff did either. When I entered the hospital, I was given a battery of intelligence, psychological and physical tests, and I surmise that now and then I saw a doctor, although I am not sure about that.

When I left the hospital, I closed my eyes, hoping to erase forever the vision of those barred windows. I vowed that I would never see the inside of another mental hospital as long as I lived—and I managed to keep that vow for about 25 years. For this period of my life, I have a fragment of a poem:

> *I dreamed I was mad one night*
> *And when I awoke, it was true.*

How do you put yourself together after six months of madness? After shocks and convulsions and barred windows and spinal taps and paraldehyde and forced dances with men who are no saner than you are? (I forgot to mention that every Saturday, the men and women were brought together for a little socializing—was this to represent reality?) I was advised to take a job requiring hard physical labor, so I went to work in a war plant where bomb casings were made. I worked there as a lathe operator for six weeks—two weeks on the day shift, two weeks on the swing shift, two weeks on the graveyard shift. The noise of the machines, the difficulty of adjusting to unnatural sleeping schedules, the feeling of being an outsider among workers who spoke their own special language—these things combined to drive me to the ragged edge of my new-found sanity, so I quit.

My illness was diagnosed as schizophrenia, or split personality, but I have since been advised that many mental illnesses were so diagnosed at that time, for the sake of convenience or because of lack of knowledge. My illness today, which has not changed much since then, is called suicidal depression with schizoid affect. I think that means that I don't want to commit suicide *all* the time, just *some* of the time.

I have a tendency to make jokes about my illness, especially its suicidal aspects. This tendency is deplored by my psychiatrist and all others associated with me therapeutically as psychologically unhealthy. But I think the reason I do this is that I don't always take my illness seriously, just as I know there are thousands of ordinary, hard-working people who don't take mental illness seriously either. If I tried really hard to be one of those ordinary, hard-working people whose values are never questioned and whose responsibilities are never shirked, maybe I wouldn't be sick. For years, I felt that my attempted suicide and hospitalization at the age of eighteen was merely a case of aggravated self-pity, and that if I had had a little more strength of character, I could have avoided the entire episode, which was painful not only to me but to my family and others who loved me. It was not until I was in my thirties and described these events to another psychiatrist that I was brought up short with the comment: "The people at the hospital obviously thought you were sick."

I have been accused of playing at suicide as at a game of Russian roulette, in which three of the chambers are loaded and I laugh as I hold the gun to my head. This would make it an act of deliberate cruelty, completely lacking in compassion. Perhaps so, but wouldn't it also be a form of madness?

As a child, my favorite game, next to jump-rope, was hopscotch, and I would loiter around the school yard after hours hoping the other girls would invite me to join their play. I find certain similarities between my life and the game of hopscotch— the magical attributes of the talisman one uses as a stone, the skill of being able to balance on one foot while performing various peregrinations, the need for strict adherence to the rules, and, above all, the disconnectedness of the whole thing.

From my home town and hospital and my first rather dismal experience with sex, I hopscotched to New York City, armed with a couple of letters of introduction, an invitation to live with a girl friend for a short time, and about $300 in cash. The letters and the encouragement to make the jump were provided by my girl friend's stepfather, Dave, who remained interested in my welfare after I was released from the hospital.

It was toward the end of September 1945 when I went to New York, and World War II was over at last. Apartments were impossible to find, but I found one; jobs were hard to get, but I got one; I took my first ride on a subway and a man dropped a rose in my lap. I was, for the first time in my life, independent, alone, and happy. I even managed to squeeze in to the opening sessions of New York University's fall term.

The apartment had three rooms and bath, and was gifted with steam heat and hot water. Its principal disadvantage was that it was on the sixth floor of a building without an elevator. It was equipped with an ice box, for which I could seldom persuade the ice man to bring me any ice. Its five flights of stairs discouraged idle visitors and discouraged me from doing much running around. It cost $26 a month and was located on the fringe of Greenwich Village, two blocks from Washington Square, where I worked by day and went to school by night.

I lived there for four years, and I remember those years as the happiest of my life. I tried suicide only once, toward the end of my sojourn, with some pills—I don't even remember what they were, probably something prescribed for sleep or headaches. I was promptly taken to the hospital where I received an injection of caffeine and was sent home. I was saying *Help!* about something, but nobody paid any attention. Suicides are a dime a dozen in New York.

I have tried and tried to analyze why those first few years in New York have such special significance for me. Whereas my first departure from home had shattered me, this second one seemed to help me breathe. Maybe the answer is that I get along well only when I am alone, that I cannot tolerate living intimately with other people, that my need for personal space extends all the way to the boundaries of whatever quarters I call home. That may be what is troubling me now. If I could just get out and live somewhere by myself, maybe I would be all right. Could I retain visiting privileges?

My happiness in my early twenties, however, derived at least in part from the processes of learning—the formal learning in university classrooms, the learning associated with my job, the extracurricular learning (I wrote a poetry column for the school newspaper), and, most important, the learning to manage my own life on my own terms, alone. I spent most of my money on books and lived on a diet of tomato soup and cheese sandwiches. I lost weight and on occasion was literally and poignantly hungry, but that did not matter. "You're too thin," my mother would say when I went home for summer vacation. Too thin? For the first time since puberty, I weighed exactly what I wanted to weigh.

There was also my sex education. My mother had informed me where babies grew and how they were born, but she had neglected to inform me how they got started. The psychiatrist I saw when I was eighteen found he had to instruct me about the sex act, beginning at the beginning. He did this with diagrams showing male and female sex organs and how they came together. "An orgasm is like a sneeze," he said. I remember feeling quite shocked about the whole thing.

In retrospect, this seems rather odd, as I had slept in the same room as my parents until the age of four or five, and it does not seem possible that I could have avoided witnessing sex in action at some point during that period. And yet, when I was sixteen, and was kissed on the mouth by a boy for the first time, I was terribly worried that I might become pregnant. Let's all bow our heads to Freud and the act of suppression.

My first lover was a student at an Episcopalian divinity school and knew a great deal more about sex than one would expect from that sort of scholar. However, he had at one time been an actor and was very dramatic, articulate and persuasive. He was also very poor and fed me cheap sherry, on which I got stinking drunk. After a while, he bored me and our relationship shriveled, along with my interest in Episcopalianism. The main thing I learned from him was how to masturbate—something the psychiatrist had omitted from his lessons.

My first husband was the son of a very orthodox Jewish family. When he declared his intention of marrying me, his mother threatened to throw herself out of the window, and his father said he would wipe his name from the list of his children. But all these pronouncements turned Henry's heart to stone (as God must have hardened the heart of the Pharaoh), and his determination to marry a "goy" became more inflexible than ever. Besides, he said, they would never carry out their threats.

Perhaps Henry was right, but I wanted no part in this catastrophe, real or intended, and I offered to convert to Judaism and become a proper Yiddisher hausfrau. Judaism is not a proselytizing religion in the first place, and Henry's mother did not help matters much by sending me to a rabbi who had not performed a conversion in seven years and who was a refugee from Nazi Germany. His first remarks to me were: "Are you prepared to see Long Island become a huge concentration camp?" "How will you react when your neighbors spit on you for being a Jew?"

My motivation for embarking upon the marriage must have been as strong as my intended husband's, for I persuaded this suspicious, cynical old gentleman (who turned out to be immensely kind) that I was a suitable candidate for Judaic womanhood. He taught me the rules and rituals of Jewish housekeeping, cooking, holiday-making, religious exercises, and wifely duties. When I had mastered these elements to his satisfaction, I was taken to a mikvah, a sort of Jewish bathhouse, where the conversion ceremony was performed. I disrobed and descended into a pool of water about four feet square and neck-deep. I dunked my head three times and repeated the ritual words in Hebrew which averred that I renounced Christ and all his teachings and adopted those of Jehovah; I also declared I would keep my household and my body in accordance with the instructions of Judaism. All of this was witnessed by three rabbis (modestly, through a tiny window in the door), who then signed a certificate declaring that I had become a bona fide Jew. As I have never renounced any of this, I suppose I still am.

Henry and I were married in accordance with Jewish ritual in the apartment of the rabbi who had performed the conversion. Henry's parents were there, and my mother, scared and bewildered, had come east for the wedding, declaring that for me to become a Jew was better than for me to have no religion at all. Prior to the ceremony, Henry lifted my veil to ascertain that he was getting the right bride (a custom stemming from the trick played on Isaac when he was given Leah instead of Rachel after seven years' hard labor); the marriage was duly sanctified under a canopy (signifying togetherness), and the wine glass was satisfactorily shattered under the heel of Henry's right foot (a gesture whose meaning has been lost to me). Following the ceremony, as we had no need to become better acquainted physically after living together for two years, Henry and I went to the movies.

I discovered almost immediately that not only did Henry not want a Jewish housewife, but he was no more interested in maintaining an orthodox Jewish household than a Japanese prime minister. We did install a mezuzah on the front doorpost, but that was the only outward admission he made of his heritage. A mezuzah is a small hollow plaque containing certain verses from the Old Testament inscribed on parchment; it commemorates the final plague visited upon the Egyptians by God when the Angel of the Lord slew all of the first-born except those in the specially marked houses of the Jews.

I was not allowed to keep a kosher kitchen with its separate sets of dishes for meat and for dairy foods and its special china intended solely for use during Passover, nor was I allowed to light Sabbath candles or attend religious services (although I had studied Hebrew in order that I might understand some of this). Despite my conversion, I was never actually accepted as a real Jew by the members of Henry's family. His grandfather, the Patriarch and a kosher butcher, never spoke to me; his father never visited our apartment; and when his mother and sister did visit, they would eat only fruit, as anything else might be contaminated by having been in contact with unkosher foods or vessels (the fruit could be washed just before eating). His aunts and uncles and cousins treated me cordially, but always as an outsider.

That I could not become a practicing Jew and that I was not accepted as a full member of the family hurt me deeply, for I think now that one of my reasons for entering into this marriage was to become a part of a living, 6000-year-old tradition that would give some meaning to my life. As it was, I participated only on the fringe. I baked the challah (Sabbath bread made with eggs and decorated with a braid running along the top); I attended Passover dinners at the home of my parents-in-law, and I remember with particular fondness the glass of wine that was always set out for Elijah. Henry and I had been married on Christmas day, so that we always had an especially festive Channukah.

Henry, on the other hand, delighted in defying Jewish customs. One of his favorite practices was to walk through the Jewish East side, where he had been born, on Yom Kippur, eating a ham and cheese sandwich. Yom Kippur is a day of absolute fasting, and of course Jews are not permitted to eat ham.

One might call this marriage another in the series of contradictions. I married Henry in order to embrace a meaningful tradition; he married me in order to contravene it. The marriage lasted seven years. I worked most of that time, writing and doing research, for the Government of Pakistan; Henry flunked out of two law schools and failed in two business ventures. It was not that he was unintelligent; it was that he used his intelligence to outwit the rules rather than to succeed within them, and he was usually caught at it. He devised ingenious ways to cheat on exams and undercut competitors, but he was bored when the only way to achieve a goal was straightforwardly.

During our marriage, I attempted suicide twice, the first time with a razor blade from which I still bear the scar. Henry found me in the bathroom and took me around the corner to a very uninquisitive doctor who accepted our story that I had cut my wrist when the knife slipped while I was trying to slice a bagel. The second time, I closed the kitchen door and turned on all the gas jets of the stove, putting my head in the oven. Once again, Henry discovered me and walked me around Manhattan until I stopped feeling dizzy and looking blue. On neither occasion did I seek psychiatric counsel, for I was afraid that a doctor would put me in a hospital, and I was terrified of hospitals. At no time did anyone recognize that attempted suicide is a cry for help.

Was what I said then any different from what I am saying now? I don't remember such dark despair, but I was surely a very unhappy woman, suffering from what would probably have been identified as a psychological depression. I felt trapped and lonely, moving in meaningless circles. But whereas then I found a way out of my trap, today I see none. My trap is my body itself, which is a heavy thing, lifeless and stupid, pulling me down into a dull, grey fog. The only way out is to get rid of it.

I left Henry in November of 1956, just one month short of our seventh wedding anniversary, taking with me my cat, my piano, my books and clothing, and moving into a large studio apartment on the upper West Side of Manhattan. The reasons for the dissolution of the marriage are rather hard to explain. I felt strongly that I was not being allowed to grow, that the marriage and/or Henry were stifling me. I compared myself to a plant whose roots were bound in a pot too small. My job with the Government of Pakistan frequently required me to work late or be out of town, and Henry resented these extra obligations. Often, on returning from a business trip, I would find that he had engaged in some petty larceny—a small theft, a bit of business trickery, or some such thing, as if he were proving something, I'm not quite sure what.

What he wanted from me basically was the Yiddisher hausfrau without the religious embroidery. He wanted me to be home every evening, to wax and polish the floors and furniture once a week, to do all the grocery shopping and to have dinner on the table at the appointed time, whether he was there or not—and frequently he was not. On the other hand, I was not allowed to do any personal shopping whatever. Henry bought every garment I wore, including my underwear and shoes, saying that I did not have "good taste." On this latter point, he may have been right, but I would have liked at least to accompany him on these shopping expeditions. He was a clever artist and should have been a fashion designer, but he lacked the discipline and the drive. After I left him, he became a professional gigolo for a while, boasting to me of his triumphs with older women —and younger ones, too. He eventually remarried, this time in a church and to a Presbyterian.

Many marriages have survived on much more fragile structures than ours, and it is certainly hard to discern any formidable reasons for suicide arising out of our relationship. Suicide is a desperate act. Razor blades and gas are not indulged in just for the experience. But Henry was not sadistic; he did not beat me, or come home drunk, or stay out all night with other women. Why, then, did I feel driven toward that "desperate act?" It's as though the germs of suicide lived within me, and from the age of eighteen when they appeared above the surface until recently when they flowered, they were nurtured and nourished in my own private garden. How did they start? Who planted them?

There is speculation that a tendency toward mental illness is genetic, just like tuberculosis or diabetes. There is little question that my "crazy grandmother" (my father's mother) was a depressive. She was a "mail-order bride" at 15, bore her first child (my father) at 16, followed quickly by two girls, at which point she put an end to the whole thing through the most effective contraceptive known to women, namely by saying "No." From then on, she hated men, marriage and childbirth, and built a world of fantasy around herself into which she retreated whenever she needed to. On her living room wall there hung, in an ornate frame, a magazine illustration of a large, colonial-style house surrounded by an expanse of lawn. In the corner of the picture, she had pasted photographs of herself and one of her daughters to look as if they were walking across the grass toward the house. This was the way she wanted her life to be, and this was perhaps the way it was during her long days of silence. She was a tall, impressive woman who lived well into her 80s, surviving her alcoholic husband by at least ten years. Deeply religious, she never, as far as I know, considered suicide.

My father is also alcoholic, and subject to dark moods and flashes of bitter temper. He is a lonely and unhappy man who makes liaisons with very strange women and has been in trouble with the police on several occasions. During the past few years, my meetings with him have been extremely painful. He is sensitive, but he can also be cruel, and my feelings toward him are very contradictory. I am torn by this ambivalence, which probably extends into my relationships with all men. I wanted his love so much, but never felt he cared. I was a nuisance, an object that got in the way of what he was doing. The fifth grade was as far as he got in school, and I think that all he ever wanted was to be outdoors and unencumbered.

My mother died some years ago of a heart attack, which came as no surprise, as she had had a long-standing heart condition stemming from childhood rheumatic fever. My feelings toward her were ambivalent, too. On the one hand, she was my only confidante (living as we did, I had no one else to talk to), but on the other hand, she represented the Enemy—a love/hate syndrome that was never resolved while she was alive. She was rigid in her morality, demanding, and unreceptive. When she died, I went home for the funeral, but I refused to look at her body or to cry during the ceremony. In fact, I refused to cry at all, and I sometimes wonder if I have ever accepted the fact that she is dead.

Curiously, I find that in my poetry I have written nothing of the ambivalences of love and hate, sin and virtue, life and death, sorrow and happiness, anger and pleasure, and yet it is these and similar contradictions which are tearing my soul apart and driving me to suicide. I feel that the world must be all one or the other, that there is no room for the dichotomy of Jung, that the land must be land and the sea must be sea and I cannot tolerate the existence of both at the same time and in the same place.

I have known many kinds of love: sexual, marital, maternal, and have been passionately possessed by each of them. But love contains its opposite; a whole love includes hate, just as God contains the devil. There is always the other side of the coin, but I have tried to live my life without ever turning it over, and now I am possessed by the dark side of things. I have loved, but no love has been fulfilling; I have been loved, but no love has been sufficient. I must face the deeply terrible truth that I can no longer love, or be loved. I harbor in my depths an ugliness that is beyond redemption.

A great deal has been written about the pain and travail associated with divorce, and it is a wrenching experience, no matter what the terms. My divorce from Henry was a reasonably amicable one, but I soon discovered that women regard divorcees with suspicion and men regard them as sex-starved. Henry never did understand my reasons for wanting a divorce, ultimately blaming it on the fact that we had been unable to have children, even though we had tried artificial insemination.

On one occasion after the divorce, Henry became violent. I stayed out late with one of my co-workers from the office (I was by this time working as a copywriter for an advertising agency), and on returning to my apartment, I found Henry standing at the door with a butcher knife in his hand. He was in a jealous rage, forced his way in, and swore that, if I did not come back to live with him as his wife, he would kill me. He strode back and forth across the room, his face red, his hand clutching the knife, and I curled up on the sofa, trying to be invisible, as children do when they feel the presence of the demon in the bedroom at night. I did not know whether he would use the knife or not, but I was not about to aggravate his anger with argument. If I were very, very still, he might forget about me and go away.

Finally, he stood in front of me and demanded that I return to his apartment. I bargained for time, asking him to give me until the next day to sort out my things. The idea of having sexual relations with him again made me feel sick. After he left, I shut myself up into the little cupboard/kitchen and turned on all the gas jets (apparently, I preferred to kill myself rather than let him do it). Unfortunately, the building was not very well constructed, and soon all of my neighbors were hammering on my door. I don't think they were as concerned about the danger to me as they were about the danger to them—after all, the gas might explode.

When the next day arrived, so did Henry, but with an apology instead of a butcher knife, and although he contacted me frequently after that, he never again attempted or threatened violence. Even after I had remarried and moved to California, Henry found out where I was and called me at least once a year to "find out if I had had a baby yet." The calls stopped coming before the baby arrived.

I have a theory that the magic number in my life is nine—the period of gestation among humans. I was almost nine when my brother was born; I was eighteen when I was first hospitalized; my relationship with Henry lasted for nine years (counting the two years we lived together before we were married). The wedding band I currently wear is dated 1959 (although Dave and I were not married until 1961), and it first became necessary for me to consult a psychiatrist in 1968—could that mean that I should have made my nine-year jump to another island then, instead of trying to stick it out? Or perhaps it will require nine years for me to recover from this illness. If that's the case, I don't know which will run out first, me, or the money to pay the medical bills.

I have a number of faults that some people label virtues. For one thing, I am always on time, much to the dismay of many party hostesses. For another, I am incapable of infidelity within the context of marriage. Unmarried, however, I slept with whom and when I pleased, regarding other women's husbands as fair game. In fact, I probably preferred other women's husbands because they lived on the other side of the fence marked "Forbidden." So, whereas I would not commit adultery, I did not object to participating in someone else's adulterous adventure. In a way, it was safe because it did not require a commitment.

Between marriages, I led an active, complex and frequently passionate sex life. I remember once taking an overdose of tranquilizers, although there weren't enough pills in the bottle to do any real damage. I learned from this that it takes a sizeable quantity of pills to cause death, unless they are very high-powered ones, such as prussic acid or cyanide. Also, I don't think I was very serious about the attempt. Something had happened with my lover which made me feel rejected, and my response was equivalent to a child's "I'll get even with you, I'll run away from home." When I was a child, I ran away from home only once, and my mother's reaction was so laconic that I decided running away wasn't worth much as a weapon.

Since rescuing me from my first suicide attempt, my old friend and mentor, Dave, had divorced his first wife and moved to Connecticut, where he was living with his second wife. Instead of stepdaughters, he now had a daughter of his own, of whom he was immensely proud. He had become a successful writer, publisher and literary agent. Once a week, he came into New York to take care of business affairs. If my attitude toward fidelity in marriage was highly stuffy, his was quite the opposite, and very soon after my divorce we were enjoying bed together. Fortunately, a friend of Dave's had an unoccupied apartment where we could go without fear of being discovered by Dave's wife.

Like my other lovers, Dave was much older than I—21 years older, in fact. He was a person of enormous vitality, enthusiasm, charm, deviousness, intelligence, humor and demonstrativeness. To be with him was exciting and warm and wonderful. He made me feel important, and he made me feel genuinely loved, even though there was no question, in the beginning, of a permanent relationship. We were having fun together, meeting for dinner, spending the night in each other's arms, parting at breakfast. It was "just one of those things." He had other women, and I had other men, and in time our feelings for each other would wear off and we would go our separate ways—or so we thought.

It didn't happen that way. Our nightcap stingers took longer and longer to drink; our morning partings became lingering and tearful; he made extra trips into New York and invented reasons for spending the week-end. I remember carrying loads of jonquils over to the apartment one day in spring. "I love you," they said, although we were careful not to use those words. We spent three weeks together once, each of us working on a book by day and making love by night, with the blessing, it seemed, of all the stars in the sky. We talked a lot, drank a lot, shared a lot. There seemed to be no end to our sharing, or to the completeness of our being together. It was an example of that curious fact of love which says: I must give all of myself in order to be complete.

We hadn't intended falling in love, but we did. Over a period of about two years, our involvement with each other became increasingly intense and exclusive. The spiral that had brought us together bound us more and more closely without our realizing it, until we were lovers caught in a web and unable to move without breaking something.

The first break came when Dave's wife found out about us. He had called her "Mary" so often that she became suspicious and asked questions. Upon hearing his confession at two o'clock in the morning, she phoned me. Several times. I had been a guest in her home. I had typed a manuscript for her. I had been a friend to her daughter. And I had betrayed all that, she said, by seducing her husband. She called me a great many ugly names. She told me I was destroying her and her daughter's happiness. She said she hoped I could sleep. I said nothing, for I had nothing to say. Everything she said was true.

The next day, Dave phoned to tell me he had agreed not to see me again. I held the telephone as if it were frozen in my hand and said, "All right," for, once again, I had nothing to say. The decision was being made without me. One would think that this would have been the occasion for another suicide attempt, but it did not happen. I simply could not believe that our relationship was going to end. There was too much between us, so much love, so much knowledge. It could not be cut off so abruptly.

Nor was it. Two weeks later, we were together again, but with his wife's knowledge. We tried to work out a compromise. He loved me, but he also loved her and was devoted to his daughter. He did not want to put an end to the marriage, but he did not want to relinquish me, either. Why could we not establish some sort of balance among us? People in other cultures did it.

But we were not people in some other culture. I wanted more, and she could not accept less. In the end, we nearly tore Dave in two, and he decided to move to California, where he was working on a television series. He would leave both of us behind and wait for the dust to settle.

I think a lot more dust was stirred up than was settled during that period. I don't know how often he called her, but he called me at least once a day, sent me roses for Valentine's Day, wrote me long, pornographic letters (which I still have), and in general we behaved like a pair of lovesick adolescents, which I guess is what we were. This was the man who had taught me sexual fulfilment. With him, I experienced my first orgasm during intercourse, and learned that sexual giving was not something a woman need be ashamed of. In bed with him, I could be who I was and not be afraid to yield to passion. I had not been capable of these things with any other man, and now he was gone and I was convinced he could not be replaced.

But I was ambivalent. One night I went out with a man of whom I was extremely fond (and Dave knew this) and did not get home until three o'clock in the morning. Dave had been trying to phone me, but had abandoned the attempt before I got back to the apartment. He phoned the next day in great distress and asked me to marry him. I thought this was a joke and said Yes, but I'd have to get some time off from my job. He said to let him know which flight I would take.

I still worked as an advertising copywriter, and my first novel was to be published later that year. I asked my boss if I could have two weeks off to go to California. He said we were too busy and the answer was No. That night I called Dave and told him I was sorry, but I could not come just yet. To which Dave replied, "What the hell are you talking about? I want you to quit your job and come out here and live with me. I've already found a house."

It was then I realized he was serious. The next day I went into the office and told my boss I was resigning in order to go to California and get married. He knew Dave and, looking at me incredulously, said, "It'll never work, Mary; it'll never work." I wept a little then, but his words had no more effect upon me than the motes in a sunbeam. My relationship with Dave was the right one, the only one, and whatever was required to insure it would be done.

In two weeks, I had sold the possessions I could not take with me, packed the ones I could (I had to part with my beloved piano, but was able to take the cat), said goodbye to everyone and everything I cared for in New York, and set off for Southern California.

Dave met the plane, drove me to a little tiny house he had rented in Burbank (which smelled, believe it or not, of orange blossoms), carried me over the threshold, tossed me on the bed, and we made love. We were together, breathing the same air. I can still remember how the sun was shining in that room, even though the blinds were drawn. The past had dissolved and there was only the present. I lay beside him, not dreaming, not caring, not thinking. He was the man I loved, the only man I had ever truly loved; I was with him and that was sufficient.

I write all this through a veil—a veil of tears, of unbelief, of grief, of incredulity, of fine tissue paper, of a feeling that thickens around me like glue and another feeling that is as unreal as the laughter of an elf. Did all this happen the way I am saying it did? And there's more, there's incredibly more. Is this how I got from there to here? If that is true, then I should be able to flap my arms and fly like a moth. I got from that island to this one, and I'm still on this one. I've tried like hell to get off this one, but I'm still on it. Moreover, there are people who are trying to tell me that this isn't a series of islands at all, that it's all one solid piece of land that begins where my father squirted his sperm into my mother's vagina and the resultant union became me. Well, do you want to know something, God? Do you want to know something, whoever's responsible for this fucking universe? I wish my father hadn't done it. I WISH HE HADN'T DONE IT!

That little house in Burbank was happiness. The life we lived there was fun and crazy and unbelievable, and when I think that I have brought our life together from that to this, I despise myself for carrying along my suitcase of sorrow and the heritage of my lunatic grandmother and my inoperable illness. We dreamed of a house on a hill looking out over a gentle meadow and we thought we had won it, but it was as unreal as that picture in my grandmother's living room and I am truly her descendant, but far more destructive.

Dave's wife and daughter also came to California, and during the summer, we had a kind of *ménage à trois*. They lived in the northern part of the state, I lived in the southern, and Dave commuted twice a week. We were all too grimly determined to make it work, but it developed into a kind of contest to see who could maintain her poise longer. Dave still wanted to protect his marriage, to be an intimate part of his daughter's life. I tried to understand this, but I also resented it, and his wife was near despair. We were all relieved when the summer came to an end and the entire troop returned to the East where, it seemed, the situation would reach some sort of resolution.

Dave's wife insisted that he consult a psychiatrist before deciding on a divorce; she believed that his infatuation with me was a temporary aberration which would correct itself with time and/or therapy. She selected the therapist—and I am reminded that it was Henry's mother who chose the rabbi to convert me to Judaism, thereby making my first marriage possible. Once again, a decision affecting my future was being made without my participation.

From September through Thanksgiving, the *ménage à trois* continued—wife and daughter in Connecticut, mistress in New York City, Dave shuttling back and forth and visiting the psychiatrist three times a week. We waited, or rather we hovered over the inevitable, as observers at a rocket ship launch count down the seconds before blast-off. The explosion came at the end of November when Dave made a final break with his wife. The divorce was granted, Dave and I returned to our wee house in Burbank, and the psychiatrist ran off to Tahiti with his mistress. That was fourteen years ago. Since then, we have all made peace—although I have no further details about the psychiatrist.

The succeeding years were active ones. We traveled, mostly by car; we entertained; I learned to replace my love for the mountains with a love for the sea; Dave bought a horse. We drank a lot, talked a lot, wrote a lot. I had three more novels published.

We met interesting people. We loved. I guess you would call it idyllic.

But there was a flaw in it somewhere, and I was afraid. Early in 1963, I learned about a program being conducted under the auspices of Stanford University to study the effects of LSD-25 on normal people. A friend of ours had participated in the program and had been so impressed and altered by it that he had written a book called *The Discovery of Love*. Dave was somewhat reluctant about my taking part in the program, but he finally agreed and took me to inquire about the details.

I was interviewed by a psychologist, examined by a doctor, and given a final screening by the psychiatrist who was in charge of the program. I told him about being hospitalized when I was eighteen, but I did not reveal the intervening suicide attempts. He was unsure at first, but I won his acceptance by saying that perhaps LSD would enable me to understand that experience and the nature of my illness. Also, he was particularly interested in the use of LSD in the treatment of alcoholics, and I admitted that I had an alcohol problem. In fact, when I told the staff how much I smoked and drank in the course of a day, they wondered how I had time to do anything else.

The next step was a series of psychological tests, beginning with the Minnesota Multiphasic Personality Inventory (MMPI), a lengthy yes/no test in which the same questions are repeated any number of times with different phraseologies so that you can't fool the computer. There were also two tests designed by the staff, one in which I was requested to rank value statements into groups of five (statements such as "Love is the most important of all emotions"), and another in which I ranked a series of rather more esoteric statements in terms of their meaningfulness to me (such as "Behold, I am come home unto myself").

There followed four sessions, spaced a week apart, using a gas called carbogen, which is a combination of 70% oxygen and 30% carbon dioxide. It is administered through a mask and at first causes very rapid, difficult breathing, almost hyperventilation. That passes after a moment, and one is plunged into some other world which I would call the unconscious, or subconscious. Each session lasted half an hour, and I was attended at all times by a psychologist and a doctor. I was instructed to express whatever I felt, whether it was to laugh or cry, to scream or moan, in addition to speaking whatever words came into my mind.

These carbogen sessions were frightening and dramatic, explosive in their impact. The gas had its effect almost immediately, and it was like bursting into a room inside myself of which I had previously been completely unaware. My eyes were closed, but I "saw" visual images of startling clarity, and I became totally involved with what I saw, frequently crying and moaning, and sometimes laughing with the carefree abandon of a child. With each session, more doors were opened, more rooms revealed. The emotions I felt were intense, and I was unable to restrain my weeping or my screaming or my joy.

During the very first session, I experienced what mystics have called the "eye of God." It was just that: an eye, looking at me. And it was terrifying, for it could see everything there was to see about me, all my faults and ugliness and the secret rottenness that I didn't want to acknowledge. I was afraid of its judgment, for I knew that my failings were far heavier on the scale than my virtues. It was an eye that would never sleep, never excuse, never forgive.

I acquired two important bits of knowledge about myself with the aid of carbogen. The first concerned a fear of mine that was so deep it would be called a phobia, I guess. It was a fear of tubes. Not tunnels, but tubes too small to stand up in. In some of the elementary schools I attended, the fire escapes from the second floor were in the form of tubes, and I was so scared I might have to go down one of these that, on days when there were to be fire drills, I refused to go to school. Later, as an adult, I went with Henry to the fun house at Coney Island, where one could slide down a long, narrow, curving tube onto a revolving turntable. We climbed the stairs in a line of people, but when we reached the top and it was our turn to go down the tube, I refused to go. Nothing Henry said and no amount of impatience expressed by the people behind us could persuade me to enter that tube. Eventually, I went back down the stairs, having to squeeze past all of the people who were moving in the other direction.

I discussed this fear with the psychologist, and he suggested that I try to imagine going through the tube while under the influence of carbogen. I was very frightened, but agreed to try. Almost at once, I found myself inside a dark but roomy place. It was lined with some soft, spongy material, and I was very contented to be there, chuckling and humming, curled in the fetal position. I did not actually experience emerging from the "tube," but I did feel that someone picked me up by the ankles. In retrospect, I believe that I was remembering my mother's womb and that my fear of tubes represented a fear of being born. Birth may be hard on the mother, but it's hard on the baby, too.

My other significant experience also concerned babies. Up until that time, I had never been pregnant, and, as I was approaching forty, I thought I would probably never have a child. I felt sad about this, and discussed it with the psychologist. He asked me to "image" a baby as I inhaled the gas. This I did, but the image of the baby quickly became white and shapeless and faded away. Then I saw a pattern of wriggly black lines, like tiny tadpoles, on a pure white background. They were in motion, going toward an egg-shaped, colorless object which had a kind of fringe around it, like eyelashes, acting as a protective barrier. I cradled my cheek against my hand and said, "Lots of little ones, lots of little ones, oh so many."

This may sound far out, but I believe the tiny tadpoles represented sperm cells and the egg-shaped object was a female ovum, namely mine, which was rejecting the sperm. Further, I believe my internalization of my mother's fear of pregnancy literally prevented my becoming pregnant, as the image suggested. It was not until two years later that I understood this and confessed it to my husband. When I did that, something within me relaxed, my ovum admitted a sperm cell, and lo! I was pregnant. One month after my fortieth birthday, I gave birth, by Caesarian Section, to an 8½-pound boy.

But opening the doors to the unconscious is a tricky and sometimes dangerous business. After the third carbogen session, my "eye" began to haunt me. I saw it in the folds of my bedclothes when I settled down to go to sleep. I saw it when I closed my eyes in the shower, and it continued to frighten me. During my final CO_2 session, I saw a vision of a woman, and I knew her, knew her not as a person but as a profound being, a cosmic symbol. She was the ultimate woman, the divine mother. "I know you," I said when I saw her. *"I know you.* I KNOW YOU." The experimenters felt then that I was ready for LSD, which would extend the experiences I had been having with carbogen, and they scheduled my LSD session for the following week.

But I began having hallucinations ahead of schedule. Trees took on weird, threatening shapes at night, and I could not sleep. I became frightened and talked to the psychologist on the phone. In the circumstances, he questioned the advisability of my proceeding with the experiment, but we decided that I should come on the designated day and we would see how things looked then. On that day, as the hallucinations had not been repeated, we elected to go ahead.

On the night before taking LSD, I was not allowed to take a drug of any kind, including aspirin, and, of course, no alcohol. I was very nervous. We were staying in a motel near Stanford, and Dave and I walked around the block several times before going to bed. I did not go to sleep for a long time, but lay looking out of the window watching the traffic move along the highway.

At eight o'clock the next morning, I was ushered into the LSD-room, which was a large, pleasant room, furnished rather like an ordinary living room with a long sofa, several comfortable chairs, a coffee table, lamps, all that sort of thing. On the walls were hanging prints of religious paintings representing the major religions of the world. The atmosphere was one of security, but I was terribly frightened. A large window at one end of the room invited me to throw myself through the glass.

I was given 200 micrograms of LSD, diluted in water. It was presented to me in a small silver chalice, and I looked at it for a long time before swallowing it. I lay down on the sofa and put a sleep shade over my eyes. Through a pair of earphones I listened to music from time to time, and some of the music I heard on that day still affects me deeply. A microphone was suspended around my neck, and everything I said was recorded on tape (those tapes have since been destroyed). The psychologist and the doctor who had been with me during the carbogen sessions were again present, and remained with me all day. This was important, as I had built up a strong trust with them, and I was going to need that trust, for LSD sometimes induces paranoid feelings.

It seemed a long time before anything happened, and when it did, it was slow and gentle, quite unlike the abrupt and explosive experience I had had with carbogen. The LSD experience also had greater continuity, was less intense, lasted longer (eight hours), and had more highs, more lows and more problems. In the beginning, I sank into myself and my body withered and died, but I did not find this frightening—my body was simply irrelevant. There were the usual visual distortions: the rug moved into great mounds, across which I could not possibly have walked; the food brought in for lunch looked moldy and maggoty; the rose I was given at the end of the day drooped and died in my hand. My hearing became painfully acute, as did my sense of touch. Several times, I caught a glimpse of a cat in the room, and once I was convinced that my hair was on fire.

But all these things don't seem to be particularly meaningful, except as they reflect on our definition of reality. Only two things happened which are germane to the thesis of this book. I had what is called a "peak experience": I gave birth to the world and everything in it. I actually pushed down with my hands and pelvic muscles until I had produced the world; then I populated it with all of its creatures from the graceful deer to the repulsive cockroaches, flowers and grasses and trees, toads and ants and vermin, the wild animals of the forest, the tame animals of the farm, rivers and streams and mountains. I became all women. My monthly bleeding was for all women. The vast pain in my bosom was for all women. Becoming all female things, I became a strumpet and enjoyed a strumpet's life, "jolly-wagging it up" (that was the phrase I used). From having mothered the earth, I became the earth itself, and all of my blood and all of my tears formed the rivers and oceans, washing over me and cleansing me.

Here is a quotation, taken from the tape, of what I said while I was deep in the experience: "I am so full of pain, my whole bosom is one mass of pain. Every mother . . . I am all mothers (weeps) . . . (sobbing) It is my pain for being a woman. I bleed for all women. I love for all women, too. I am my own mother. My thorn is her thorn, too. It is the thorn of all mothers for their children, for all of mankind. It's all right to be the mother of ants and scarabs and things, too. (moans and sighs) . . . and all us little cats, too."

The "thorn" stayed with me for several years, a sharp needle-like pain near my heart which fluctuated in intensity. Electrocardiograms failed to give any explanation, but gradually the pain lessened and finally it faded away altogether. I never did understand what it meant.

If I had to summarize my peak experience in one sentence, I would say: "Behold, I am Woman." Prior to taking LSD, I disliked women. I found them tiresome, trivial, bitchy and boring. I found nothing enobling in womanhood, not even the capacity to be a mother—especially not that capacity, for my own mother had nothing noble about her. I resented the physiological aspects of woman-ness, such as menstruation, which I tried to ignore. With LSD, I found the beauty of being a woman, the tremendous compassion, the gift of creation, the immense, maternal love for all children of all kinds in all places. I came away from that day grateful that I was a woman, and I have felt differently about all women ever since.

That problem was resolved, but a second problem persisted: my relationship with Dave. During the carbogen sessions, I had spoken of him in terms of lyrical love. Under the influence of LSD, although I remembered the love, I also hated, and spoke of Dave in the vilest language I could think of. When I looked at his picture (a publicity photograph), I tore off the autograph (which was his nom de plume) and called him a homosexual because of the green eye-shadow I saw in his eyelids. I kept saying, "We shouldn't have married; it was a mistake; it was wrong." I felt our marriage was wrong in some vitally essential way, like sin. But I could not understand why I felt it was so wrong, or what I could do about it, and I felt a great anguish at the extent of my hatred for him.

About three o'clock in the afternoon, I asked if Dave could come to see me, and within a short time, he was there. As soon as I saw him, I was filled with joy and love. We embraced, and I said, "You, my rum-soaked raggle-taggle pirate, you, my devil, you are the thorn in my heart and you love me anyway." When I studied his face, it became frightened, and I wanted to still his fear. Later, his face became one of the fierce, bloodthirsty gods of Central America, painted with geometrical figures. Then it became Freud and finally a little boy frightened of his father. But none of this helped to resolve the ambivalence or the intensity of my feelings for him.

We went back to the motel about five-thirty, having made an appointment to return the following afternoon for a recapitulation. There were friends waiting for us, and we sat up and talked and drank until quite late. The next morning, I awoke feeling more joyful than I had ever felt in my life. I announced that

I was a "new woman" and that the new woman needed some new clothes. We went to a large department store, and when I walked into it, I was so overwhelmed by the beauty of the colors, the magnificence of the decor, the divinity of the people, that I could do nothing but stand there and weep. I bought the new clothes without my usual hesitations, and spent the rest of the day in a state of euphoria. Every tree, every flower, every blade of grass was exciting; so was the pavement, the asphalt, the tablecloth in the luncheonette, the candles, the waitress...

On the following day, we went home. My euphoria lasted about a week, although I began to have trouble sleeping. I had anticipated some difficulties in adjusting to the "newness" of the world around me, but I felt sure of two things: 1) that if Dave were just patient enough, I would become the best wife he had ever had, and 2) that I would never commit suicide. Today, ten years later, Dave worries about me constantly, and in the past year and a half, I have made three serious suicide attempts and have been hospitalized for psychiatric reasons four times.

After I took LSD, I said to myself: Now I am a new person; many things have been revealed to me; I understand myself and others better; I shall be able to handle problems more intelligently, more calmly; I shall be more mature. On repeating the tests I had taken before LSD, the statement, "Behold, I am come home unto myself," seemed particularly significant.

The year following the LSD-trip was one of the worst in my life. I never knew when I would start hallucinating, and the hallucinations terrified me; I could not sleep without a light burning somewhere nearby; often I could not sleep at all, because I was afraid the evil part of me would take control and kill Dave. When I did sleep, I conducted long, audible conversations with Dave (who was awake and thought that I was awake, too), which I did not remember in the morning. In those conversations, I would frequently discuss things I did not know I knew —Tiresias, for example, or Beardsley. I felt completely fragmented and jangled, unfamiliar with myself. If I had had a job requiring me to work a regular eight-hour day, I could not possibly have kept it.

I had a series of dreams in which I was a pair of twins, sometimes male and sometimes female. In every case, one of the twins was virtuous and stupid and the other was brilliant and evil. I identified with the virtuous one, but the evil one was always the stronger. We performed terrible crimes together—kidnapping, murder, dismembering infants. Finally, in the last of the dreams, the twins were Siamese, and I realized that we shared the same bloodstream, that we were two parts of a whole, two sides of a coin. Today, I still wish I could unite the brilliance and the virtue and push the stupidity and the evil under the rug, but I guess that is not possible.

For several months, I struggled with these occurrences as best I could, discussing them frequently with the psychologist or doctor who had been with me when I took LSD. I felt ashamed and inadequate because I could not tolerate the hallucinations, could not learn from them the way others had done. I felt only terror—panic, really. I was subject to attacks of sudden, overwhelming fear that washed over me and made me want to run and hide, but I had no place to run to.

Thus, it was finally decided that I had best be under the care of the psychiatrist who was in charge of the experiment. He put me on tranquilizers and met with me weekly for about six months, until he had to return to the East. He had been working with LSD for years and believed firmly in the learning possibilities it provides. At the same time, he recognized when it was necessary to put the lid on, and he helped me reestablish the boundaries between conscious and unconscious.

Interestingly enough, at no time during this period did I consider suicide. If there were a suicidal growth burgeoning in my unconscious, why did it not spring fotrh then? For that was a period of horrors, fears, hallucinations, nightmares. But I knew all that time that I could put out my hand and Dave would be

[43]

there, supporting me with his strength, his concern, his *care*.

Some two years after I took LSD, I was alone in the house and felt that I was ovulating. I could usually identify the process by a certain uterine heaviness. This time, for some reason, it frightened me, and I resolved to be careful and avoid sexual intercourse that night. Then I realized what the fear meant—I was afraid of becoming pregnant. I felt intensely ashamed. After all, I thought, a woman's purpose was to bear children; it was not something I should be afraid of.

A month or two later, I confessed all of this to Dave, and speaking the words aloud must have represented a kind of yielding on my part, for the following month we discovered that I was pregnant. "But I've never been pregnant before," I protested to the obstetrician. "There's always a first time," he replied sagely. The baby was born in December, and his coming shifted the focus of our life-style. Instead of renting houses, we bought one; instead of taking off on a trip at a moment's notice, we became sedentary, content to watch this new being, this product of our lives, as he grew and changed. For me, who had written hundreds of poems, he was a new kind of poem, and I learned a new kind of love. I held him in my arms for long hours, warmed and confirmed by his presence.

What terrible things have I done to that love, to that child of my womb? My body instinctively knew how to care for him, but I have betrayed that knowledge and instead of nurturing, I am destroying him. My child, my child, conceived in beauty and carried in joy, I cannot move now without harming you. The question is which move will harm you least. Would you not be infinitely benefitted if I gave you a new beginning? Whatever I do, you will never be able to forgive me.

In September, before the baby was born, my husband had to undergo emergency surgery for a diseased gall bladder. Although it did not show up on X-rays, a gallstone was also suspected, and the surgeon had to search for it while Dave was under anesthesia. The fact that something like this could happen to Dave, that he could be physically vulnerable making it necessary for a surgeon to cut into his body with a knife, destroyed some vital part of my faith in him. Never again could I reach out to him for support, for he too was only human, whereas the man I had married was invulnerable, indestructible, unfailingly tough.

Together with this erosion went the fear that he would die, for a friend of ours had died in similar circumstances when, during gall bladder surgery, it was discovered that his inner organs were a mass of cancer cells. I could not sleep the night before the surgery because, in my customary way of romanticizing events, I was afraid I would have to give a life for a life— Dave's life for the life in my womb.

The surgery on Dave was successful. The gallstone was found and mounted in plastic for us to put on our knick-knack shelf, and Dave came home almost as good as new. But my love for him bore a scar as disfiguring as the one on his body.

Another factor eroding our relationship was Dave's recurrent attacks of hiccups. Shortly after we were married, he began to have occasional bouts of hiccuping, mild at first and easily stopped with water or alcohol. As time went by, these attacks increased in frequency and intensity until they were almost a daily occurrence. They were not like the hiccups one reads about in the newspaper in which the victim hiccups incessantly, day and night, unable to sleep or eat. Dave was usually able to stop his hiccups with a drink of water; the problem was that they would start again in fifteen minutes or half an hour or an hour, depending upon how lucky he was that day. Also, he was almost always able to gain relief by lying down.

Over the years, the hiccups have become an intrinsic part of our lives and a source of antagonism between us. Once again, Dave has proved he is not invulnerable. Moreover, the fact that the hiccups started shortly after we were married indicates to me that he is still harboring guilt feelings about leaving his wife and daughter. In other words, it is all my fault. If he had not married me, he would be growing old in comfort and security, uncrippled by a physical problem that appears to be irremediable.

Incidentally, if you have a hiccup remedy, please don't send it to us. We have tried them all, from folk remedies such as drinking a glass of water upside down or breathing into a paper bag to sophisticated methods such as running a plastic tube down one nostril and tickling the pharynx. Dave has also tried chiropractic, hypnosis and acupuncture with no long-term benefit. In some cases, it is possible to stop hiccups by severing a nerve which runs from the diaphragm up through the back of the neck. There are two of these nerves, one on each side, and one can apparently be severed without causing any harm. It has been established, however, that Dave hiccups on both sides, making that procedure impossible.

So the hiccups arrive every day, sometimes in the morning, sometimes at noon, sometimes not until four o'clock. Sometimes they are so harsh they seem about to strangle him; other times they are gentle and slide away easily with a glass of water. Once they have started, they last until he goes to bed and sometimes they last all night, in which case he takes in so much fluid that he regurgitates everything. His medication combines a tranquilizer and an anti-depressant, and although it does not stop the hiccups altogether, it helps, for without it Dave hiccups constantly.

I have no compassion for these hiccups and am barely able to tolerate them. They jar me with their alien rhythm and throw the environment slightly off center like a picture hanging crooked. I'm not sure whether it's the picture or the room which needs straightening. In the first place, Dave's hiccups are my fault for marrying him. In the second place, if he were the man he was supposed to be, he would not have them in the first place. In the third place, they have deprived him of his vitality, his interesting-ness, his ability to write, his ability to talk to people, his interest in doing anything whatsover except sit in his chair and smoke and occasionally read a newspaper. He says that if I were to commit suicide, the bottom would fall out. Fall out of what? It doesn't seem to me there is any bottom to where he is. If I committed suicide, it would at least give him something to do. They say that when you hit bottom, they only way to go is up, but I don't think I'll ever hit bottom; there isn't any.

I guess that represents the difference between my point of view and his. Dave feels that suicide is depraved, and a lot of people would agree with him. I don't feel it is depraved, I think it's logical; when it's time to go, it's time to go.

I read an article the other day about a man who makes pottery out of the ashes of cremated humans mixed with clay, and I thought that was a lovely idea; I hope someone will do that with my ashes. Perhaps I do want to be remembered a little. "See that vase over there? It's made out of my mother." The only way I can have an impact on life is by dying.

I first started getting sick when our son was just under two years old. I was tired all of the time, I had dizzy spells, I wasn't interested in anything. My internist ran me through the usual battery of tests and the only thing he could find wrong with me was high blood pressure—not alarmingly high and amenable to medication. So every couple of months, I went in and had my blood pressure checked, but I still did not feel any better. Finally he said, "I think you're depressed." "That's silly," I said, "what do I have to be depressed about?" He shrugged his shoulders, gave me a bottle of capsules, and said, "Try these. See if they make any difference."

They did make a difference, and the next time the doctor saw me, he said, "I think you should see a psychiatrist." "No thanks," I said vehemently, all my old fears of psychiatrists and hospitals returning in a rush. After all, I reasoned, my experience with the psychiatrist after LSD had been under special circumstances; any ordinary psychiatrist would probably stick me in a hospital first thing. "Well," my doctor said, "I can't go on giving you these drugs because I don't know enough about them and their side effects."

So I went home in tears, more depressed than ever, and when Dave asked me what was wrong, I said, "Nothing. That's just the trouble."

Dave finally became so concerned that he went to see the internist, and between the two of them they set up an appointment for me to see a psychiatrist. When I was presented with this *fait accompli*, I agreed, but on two conditions: 1) that he would not toss me into a hospital, and 2) that I would like him. The psychiatrist I met that day made me feel comfortable and relaxed; he understood my fear of hospitals, and he cared. I was amused that one of the first things he had me do was take the same old MMPI test for the third time. Unlike the other doctors, however, he shared the results with me.

I consulted the psychiatrist for about a year and a half, and as it became apparent that at least some part of my problem arose from my relationship with Dave, we had joint sessions for several months. Dave, however, although he favored psychiatric treatment for me, did not feel it would help him or the two of us together, and did not cooperate. Perhaps he could not. At any rate, this left the psychiatrist with no place to go, and the sessions were terminated.

I managed to get along pretty well for several years on a maintenance dose of an antidepressant, but then all of my former symptoms reappeared, and once again I showed up in my internist's office. It was a different doctor this time, because my former doctor had died in the interim. The new man could find nothing out of order with my blood pressure, but he found things definitely askew with my liver, which he attributed to my heavy drinking.

Alcohol, of course, was the way I kept myself going. I started drinking in New York where all those beautiful ads that you see on TV and in magazines could not possibly be put together without a martini in hand. For Dave and me, it was an integral part of the day. We had a couple of drinks before lunch and, if we had guests, wine with lunch. Cocktail time started at four o'clock. Dinner was not served until seven or eight o'clock, and after dinner we would have a few nightcaps.

The doctor urged me to cut down to two drinks a day, and for a while I did, so that my next liver test turned up normal. However, my depression increased, and it wasn't long before the internist asked me when I had last seen the psychiatrist. "About three years," I said, and he suggested that I reestablish contact.

The first question the psychiatrist asked me was whether or not anything had changed in my life since the last time he had seen me. No, I told him. Then he said my depression was of a cyclic nature and that this had probably been true all of my adult life and might have accounted for some of my attempts at suicide. He told me of a new drug called lithium, which had proven extremely useful in the treatment of manic-depressives and was sometimes helpful in the treatment of depressives, although it could not be used effectively until the depressed person had recovered somewhat. He said he hoped to be able to use this drug for me, but that, in the meantime, we would have to proceed in other directions—antidepressants, sleeping pills, therapy.

Perhaps it was being told that my illness was cyclic, perhaps it was the fear that I would not recover from the depression, perhaps it was a desire for a dramatic change in my life style— whatever the reason, my depression this time was much more severe, and I became obsessed with the idea of suicide.

At home, I was almost incapacitated, accomplishing only those things which were absolutely necessary. I remember the fall of 1972 as a nightmare cast in gray—first came Halloween and the costume for my son; then came my birthday early in November; then Thanksgiving when we were always joined by my sister; early in December came my son's birthday and the required party; and finally Christmas, with all the Christmas cards, the presents, the tree, the decorations, the picture-taking, the parties.

I also became involved in volunteer activities, the idea being that if I had something to do away from home, I might feel more stimulated and enthusiastic about life in general and home life in particular. Or perhaps it was that if I did something requiring a focus outside myself, I would not feel so boxed in. But I took my box with me wherever I went, and the effort required to carry it around while engaging in my volunteer work exhausted me. I was usually in tears by the time I got home, too tired to do more than sit. In short order, I developed an ear problem requiring surgery. The otolaryngologist assured me it was a legitimate, physical ear problem, but I was convinced it was induced because I hated what I was doing and the resultant stress affected my ear. My other theory is that I was not listening, or did not want to listen, to what my psychiatrist was telling me.

The day after Christmas, I told my psychiatrist that if he did not put me in the hospital, I would commit suicide. He did not want to hospitalize me, but my threat left him no alternative. I had a small bottle of Seconal, which I then gave him, and I entered the hospital that afternoon. He told me later that the dosage would not have killed me, but that it would have caused a lot of trouble.

I don't really know how I felt then. All I know is that I could not go on living as I had been; all I was and everything I was doing had become intolerable.

At this point, I am reminded of one of the experiences I had while under the influence of LSD. I was cleaning out a septic tank by hand, and I said, "Get it out, get it *all* out. No wonder you're such a wretch with all this shit in here."

Well, I have come to the point in this book where I feel I must get it all out, but I wonder whether that "all" will be of any interest to anyone except me, for cathartic purposes, and maybe a couple of psychiatrists who are studying what goes on in the mind of a would-be suicide.

Right now, for example, at this very moment, I have a sufficient quantity of pills in my medicine chest to kill myself. Mind you, not just land in the Intensive Care Unit with tubes running in and out of me, or wake up unable to identify familiar objects because there is a possibility of brain damage, but out-and-out kill myself. Like dead, man. For good. Unless, God help us, there's something to that crap about reincarnation. All I have to do is swallow those pills tonight after everyone else has gone to sleep, and when Dave wakes up, as he frequently does, and looks over to check whether I'm there or not, I'll be there. I'll tell my son before he goes to sleep that I'm taking an extra sleeping pill, so that if I don't wake up when he comes in to tell me he's scared or has had a bad dream, it's all right. That way, I'll have all night to die, and no one will find out until six-thirty tomorrow morning when the alarm goes off.

On the other hand, I have a contract with Dave that I won't commit suicide until I have finished this book. I also have a similar contract with my doctor, but I don't think he believes in it. Nonetheless, one of the reasons I have all of those pills is that he gave them to me because he is going away for a week and had to give me twice as many pills as he normally does. If I kill myself, I can leave him with a nice, tidy little guilt feeling. Well, I can say, he took a chance and he lost; that's the way the cookie bounces. But can I swallow all those pills, plus the ones I have stashed away for just such an opportunity as this, while thinking of his office and the black leather chairs and the pictures on the walls and the transference and the dependence and all of the emotions that have been expressed within those four walls? Can I say to him, "Go fuck yourself," like that? Can I? Well, I've done it before—it just didn't come off.

And there's Dave. He won't be abe to handle it. I know that from the one time I nearly died as a result of a suicide attempt. The shock caused him to collapse, after I was "safe." He lost his sense of balance and fell down the stairs, seriously cutting his face and suffering a concussion. But he would last long enough to see to it that our son was properly cared for.

Then, of course, there is our son. He is eight years old and brilliant, very perceptive, tall, and good-looking. We quarrel a lot, and he says I am good at two things: cooking, and failing to commit suicide. I've probably already done a pretty good job of messing him up psychologically, and if I stick around, I'll fix it up for sure. On the other hand, I'm the only mother he has, and killing myself would be rejecting him. But is that the worst possible form of rejection? Personally, I don't think so; I think my father's way was a lot more damaging. My son can go and live with his half-sister and his niece and be reared in a young and healthy environment which is not addicted to alcohol or suicide.

So shall I do it? The thought gives me so much pleasure. I want to so much that it brings tears to my eyes. I could leave, I could leave tonight and never have to come back. I wish I could. I wish I could.

But I probably won't. There is still that tiny spark of life in me that won't go out. I won't be dead tomorrow, but I'll wish I were.

So, back to the hospital where I went on that bleak day after Christmas, 1972. It proved to be quite a different sort of place than the one I inhabited when I was eighteen. It occupies a wing of a modern, major hospital in our town, and is identified by the word "Psychiatry" on the door, which normally is not locked. There are no bars on the windows, but they cannot be opened because of the heating/air conditioning system. The rooms are like ordinary bedrooms with two beds to a room (not hospital beds) and private bathrooms; there is a large living room with a television set, stereo, and radio; in the dining room, the flatware is not counted; the kitchen is equipped with stove, refrigerator, sink, soft drinks, coffee urn, and so forth. The members of the staff do not wear uniforms. Your own psychiatrist comes to see you every day except Sunday.

There is group therapy once and sometimes twice a day, with the groups kept small enough to allow for full participation. Incidentally, I forgot to mention that men and women are housed in the same unit. Dance therapy, physical therapy, outings to the beach or concerts or movies are all available to the patients, and there is excellent occupational therapy equipment, including materials for work in leather, paint, ceramics, weaving. There is a volleyball/tennis court and an outdoor barbecue.

Not all patients are allowed the same privileges, of course. Some are free to come and go at will, provided they sign in and out and indicate where they are going. Others must be accompanied by a staff member, and still others are not allowed to leave the unit at all. On occasion, when a patient is greatly disturbed and possibly dangerous to himself, the main door is locked to insure that he stays in the unit. When checking in, each patient's bags are examined for medications and potentially harmful objects such as razor blades, which are confiscated.

Altogether, the unit has the atmosphere of a rest home rather than a hospital, and I think that is the way I felt about it during my first sojourn there, which lasted about three weeks. I was allowed considerable freedom, spent every weekend at home, and soon was discharged, feeling somewhat stronger.

All of my life I have written poetry, although I have never tried to have any of it published. I usually throw it away or give it away or lose it. When Dave and I first became lovers, he urged me to write a book, which I did. It was called *Tenderly, My Love*, and was essentially a long love poem. It was short on plot and the characterizations were minimal, but the language was beautiful. It received about six reviews, the most interesting of which appeared in a small, midwest newspaper, calling the book, "slime . . . iridescent slime, but slime nonetheless." I always thought that review would have made great publicity for increased sales, but the publisher did not agree with me. The reason, incidentally, the reviewer called the book "slime" was that the love relationship was an adulterous one.

All of the poetry of love and joy and heartbreak and romance that had been building up in me for thirty-odd years spilled out in that book, which was essentially about me and Dave and our love. As a book, it was a total commercial failure, but as an expression of sensual feeling, it represented some kind of epitome for me.

After returning from the hospital in January, 1973, I began to write a new kind of poetry, profuse and evocative, but on another subject: death. During that period, I felt as if I were a passenger on a ship of life, an unwilling, even an unreal passenger. I did not know the ship's destination, nor did I wish to know. I did not know the ship's other passengers, nor did I wish to know. Perhaps some of them were potential suicides, like me; perhaps some of them were brimming with a joy of life—a life I could not endure; perhaps some of them were merely passengers and didn't much care, just going along for the ride, you might say. Whenever I felt myself to be one of those passengers, I wanted to get off.

My feelings toward Dave reached a low point equivalent to the high they had achieved when I wrote *Tenderly*. I felt that I was married to a dead man, that he was no longer making any contribution to our marriage, that he was rattling around inside himself as I was rattling around inside myself, and that we no longer had any communication.

I wrote extensively of the pain I felt, of the feeling that although I might appear to be calm and capable on the surface, inside I was insane. I have always feared that my psyche, by which I mean the structure of my personality, was fragile, and in those early months of 1973, my psyche began to crack. Worse, I could not see any way of patching it, let alone making it whole. I felt I had to sit quietly, holding it together, or it would break apart, and all the ugly things in it would spill out all over the floor.

On re-reading those poems, I find two things predominate. On the one hand, I was fighting my suicidal impulses, trying to put them down, push them aside. On the other, I felt that my interior was so infested with malignancy that the world would be better off without me.

I usually wrote the poems at night while I was trying to go to sleep, and I read them to Dave in the morning over our several cups of tea. Whether he recognized them for what they were, I do not know. At any rate, he did not push any alarm buttons. On March 17th, I wrote: "Last week, I was insane. This week, I am scared and sick. What—and where—will I be next week?"

On Sunday night, March 18th, I took an overdose of Fiorinal and Chloral hydrate and was taken to the hospital and placed in the psychiatric unit, apparently all right but unconscious. During the night, the bottom fell out of my blood pressure, and I was moved to the Intensive Care Unit where I remained for about twelve hours. When I was returned to the psychiatric unit, I was still not fully conscious and was equipped with a catheter and a full-time special nurse. Despite the catheter, I continually tried to get out of bed to go to the bathroom and usually fell down. I was very much out of focus and could not answer simple questions such as: "Where are you?" "What day of the week is it?" "What month is it?" I remember looking out of the window to see if there were any snow on the ground; in southern California, that was not a very astute method of determining the season. These interviews were conducted by my own psychiatrist, and although I think I was able to identify him immediately, it took me some time to identify the ring of keys he held in his hand.

There was obviously some possibility of brain damage, and as soon as I could be disconnected from the catheter and sit up straight in a wheelchair, I was given an electroencephelograph test. EEG for short. At first, I was terrified of having my brain wired to a machine, as if some of the substance would be drained off, but after having four EEGs, I decided they were, on the whole, rather fun.

First of all, tiny clips joined to wires of many colors were fastened to my scalp. They pinched a little at first, but then there was no pain. The differently-colored wires were attached to a recording device, and the attendant was attached to this device, too. I mean by this that the attendant in this case was so impassive she gave the impression of being just another little wire.

I have forgotten the exact sequence of events, but it went something like this: I lay down on the bed with a flat pillow under my head and a light cover over my body. I was told to relax and then to hold my eyes open, without blinking, until the attendant gave a signal that it was all right to blink. This period of time was longer than I could normally hold my eyes open without blinking, and I was proud when I managed to do it, although I could feel the strain of doing something unnatural. All of the time, little gongs were ringing, pens were busily drawing lines all over a large sheet of paper, and the attendant occupied herself making notes and checkmarks here and there. My brain was being recorded.

The eye-blinking test was repeated several times. Then I was asked to close my eyes, and bright lights were flashed over them, beginning very slowly and increasing in speed until they were flashing extremely rapidly. What was interesting about this test were the colors I saw. At first, there was an ordinary white light, but as the flashing increased in speed, the colors changed, settling into predominantly one color or another, although the color of the light itself was always the same. The first time I was given the test, I think the color I saw was primarily blue, but it was different in each test. Whether or not that had anything to do with the condition of my brain, I do not know. The net effect was one of exhilaration. However, in another part of the test, I was asked to hyperventilate (breathe very rapidly), which made me cold and dizzy, and that was the end of the exhilaration.

(Now, for those of you who tuned in for today's episode, you will note that I did not commit suicide last night. The spark of life may have had something to do with it, but there was also the fact that the doctor did not after all provide me with enough pills to do the job. He made a mistake, a miscalculation, based, perhaps, on his own reluctance to knowingly supply me with the wherewithal for death. It's too bad, really, for now I'll never know whether I would have taken them.)

My first EEG indicated that all was not right with my brain, but a week later I scored normal. "No scrambled brains," said the doctor. Later, when a high-powered antidepressant brought undesirable side effects, a third EEG gave an abnormal reading. After a week without the troublesome drug, however, the EEG report was "within the normal range," which I suppose is something to cheer about. My mind doesn't seem to function "within the normal range."

This time I was in the hospital for two months and came to know the place pretty well. I grew bold enough to participate in group therapy, and I learned to paint—I, who had never held a paint brush in my hand and firmly believed I could not draw. I became so entranced with painting that I later took evening classes. I had days of despair and days of calm, following the routine without protest, as obedient as ever. In the beginning, my activities were restricted, but as time went by I was given more and more freedom until I had lunch dates two or three times a week outside the hospital. But no matter how socially active I might be, the hospital was my base and represented safety. There, I could try to learn to cope with my interior stresses without, at the same time, having to cope with problems imposed from outside. If, now and then, I felt brave enough to emerge into the outside world, it was with the knowledge that the hospital was always available as a retreat.

It seems, in my case at least, that acute depression must be accompanied by some physical problem. On the previous occasion, it had been my ear; this time, I developed arthritis in my neck so severe at times that I could not hold my head straight. It was treated with traction and massage and improved greatly during my hospitalization, as I guess my state of mind did, too.

I remember many faces from those eight weeks, many voices, many scenes. I do not recall a single instance of indifference on the part of the staff, and I remember many when I received the warmth and understanding and generosity I needed. For the first time in my life, outside the psychiatrist's office, to be mentally ill was not considered ugly or contemptible. I developed a deep affection for one of the other patients, an affection which arose at least in part from our sharing of the same suicidal disease. Such friendships usually do not survive the hospital environment, but they are important within it, and I shall always be grateful for the role she played in my life.

I was discharged in the middle of May, resolved, if not prepared, to give some coherence to my life. Dave and I agreed to participate in something we called "family therapy," for want of a better name, with two members of the hospital staff, and we began meeting with them weekly. During my absence, our son had refused to visit any of his friends at their homes, confessing he was afraid something might happen to his father while he was away and then he would be truly an orphan. It took him some time to get over this fear, but by the middle of June, we were able to leave him with some old friends while we took a short trip. I am afraid this trip did not improve my mood much, for a poem I wrote then states: "It is sad to live," and "God weeps that I cannot die."

My sister visited us that spring and again later. I wish I could include here the many times I talked with her, the many times she soothed me, the many times she listened to my despair, my fear and my forsakeness. Seventeen years younger than I, she is in many ways much wiser.

I spent much of the summer at the beach, usually with my son and one or more of his playmates. As I sat on the sand, sounds floated past without touching me and my presence sifted away into the sea. The sea was my mother, my torment and my peace, and I longed to be united with it. I tried to express this feeling in my paintings and poetry.

The poems I wrote that summer contain a growing message of helplessness, a feeling of not being present, of being lost somewhere in the fog with no trail to follow and no clues to guide me. I did not struggle as hard against suicidal feelings as I had previously, for I felt I was already partly obliterated. "I am here,"

I wrote, "only when someone is looking at me."

But one day I discovered that "someone" was *not* "looking at me." It was dramatic and frightening, and it came about as a by-product of psychotherapy. For as long as I could remember, I had had the feeling of being watched. I cannot say whether this feeling came from the idea of God, who notes even the falling sparrow, or from the idea that my mother always knew what I was doing, especially when it was wrong. Whatever the reason, it was a very strong feeling and often affected the way I behaved. No, I would say to myself, I mustn't do that for someone is watching. Or, Did my watcher notice how expertly I parked the car?

This was not the watcher spoken of as a witness in some religious doctrines. That witness does not judge. My watcher was always identified as a specific individual, someone I had known in the past, who was following my movements by means of some mechanical device. And, of course, my watcher judged.

One day that summer I realized I wasn't being watched any more. It gave me a strange feeling, partly freedom and partly loneliness, raising the question of who was the watcher and who was the watched. I grew afraid; I thought that if no one was watching, it was because there was nothing to watch. Inside, I was empty. People like my psychiatrist were looking for whatever was inside me and it was all a huge joke; there was nothing there.

It's true, too; I am empty. I have nothing inside, nothing to give, nothing to say. I sat on the patio one day recently having drinks with my husband and I said, "I don't love you. It is impossible for me to love anyone now." As for my son, I do not deserve to love him. Not only am I unworthy of his love, but I am also unworthy of feeling the beauty of loving him. To love is to give, and I can give nothing because I have nothing, I am nothing. Any gift I offer would be as empty of meaning as I am.

During those summer months, my husband was in charge of my medication. He carried it around in his pocket in the daytime, and at night he usually put it in the pocket of his robe or in a dresser drawer or somewhere. At about four o'clock in the morning on September 16th, I woke him and asked for a sleeping pill. I had been drinking heavily and often could not sleep in such circumstances. Having established the whereabouts of the pills, I waited for Dave to go back to sleep and then swallowed them all. There were a great many (about 150), as several of the prescriptions had just been refilled. At nine o'clock, when he awoke, I was unconscious but still breathing.

Once again, an ambulance carted me off to the hospital, where it was met by my therapist and my medical doctor. I was immediately placed in a respirator in the Intensive Care Unit and equipped with intravenous feeding tubes and catheters and I don't know what else. For three days I remained in a coma, but on the fourth day I was transferred from ICU to the medical unit, complete with catheters, IV's and around-the-clock nursing. When I woke up, it was just like waking from a long sleep and I felt curiously refreshed and completely unaware of the activity that had been going on around me. Because of the drug involved (Triavil), I had none of the previous drifting in and out of consciousness, none of the struggle to relate to the present. The first time I was conscious of seeing my psychiatrist, I said brightly, "That's a key ring."

This was the suicide attempt which threw Dave into shock. Apparently he managed all right for the first few days, but by the time the neighbors found out what was going on and my sister was able to come, his sense of balance was so askew that he could hardly walk across the room. On Saturday, September 22nd, he fell down the stairs from the second floor to the first, cutting his face badly and suffering a concussion. Now it was his turn to be taken to Intensive Care.

The cut was a deep one, going through his eyebrow and down his nose, but the surgeon who repaired it did a masterly job, for today the scar is not discernible. No reason could be found for Dave's loss of equilibrium, other than shock, and he was moved into the regular medical ward at the end of the second day.

By the time this accident occurred, I was in the psychiatric unit, still watched over by special nurses, but something had to be done about caring for our son, as my sister could not remain with us indefinitely. I discussed the problem with my psychiatrist, and we agreed that, as I was functioning fairly normally, I would return home and go into intensive psychotherapy (daily meetings) rather than remain in the hospital. "I feel like Miss Shit-ass of 1973," I declared.

Dave returned home at the end of the week, and we were now heading into the Fall merry-go-round, beginning with the school fair, then Halloween, my birthday, Thanksgiving, our son's birthday and Christmas. I dreaded the whole thing, but this year it was to be different. I bought very few presents and wrote no Christmas letters, which was a relief, for Christmas letters are supposed to be full of joy and cheer, and I had none of those things in me, not anywhere at all. I despised Christmas for forcing me to put on a false face. We spent the Christmas holidays in the East with Dave's daughter and her family and her mother. It was our son's first experience with snow, and a refreshing change for all of us.

During that fall I was also occupied with yoga classes and my class in painting. Another occupation was wine, much to the distress of my psychiatrist, because, on occasion, after a certain amount of wine, I became suicidal. The psychiatrist asked me not to drink so much, and I agreed, but drank so much anyway, which he regarded as a breach of trust, which I guess it was. It was also an example of my inclination to cross barriers that are set up in front of me.

When we returned from our Christmas holiday, I found that nothing had changed and life would go on as before. I would get up at six-thirty to get our son ready for school and drive him to meet his school bus. Then I would return home, practice my yoga exercises, drink my tea and read the paper. The day died right there.

Everything I did was done from the bottom of the place where I lived, where one was never concerned about the weather and where no one ever came to visit because there was no way to get there. When anyone touched me, it was through a kind of veil, and conversation took place through this veil, too. The only real communication was tears—"I start my day with a washing," I wrote—and nobody seemed to understand these. The only real feeling was pain which could only be assuaged with wine.

I felt completely unrelated to what I was doing and what was going on around me, and the desire for death was once again uppermost in my mind. I wrote of my hope for death, my eagerness for it, as if death were my lover, calling to me from the middle of some forest, the bottom of some sea. It should be easy to die. People die all the time, quickly, suddenly, softly. Is it always so hard? Is that final moment, that final breakthrough always so difficult to achieve? I longed for a split second of complete insanity, just long enough to open the vein, fire the gun, drive the car off the road.

Since the previous September, the psychiatrist had been in charge of my medication, giving me only the pills I needed from one visit to the next. Therefore, on the 28th of January, I told him of my new suicide plan, which did not require pills. I would take the vacuum cleaner hose, hook it onto the exhaust pipe of the car, run it in through the car's rear window, and turn on the motor. Then I would sit in the back seat with a bottle or two of wine and go to sleep, hopefully for the last time. I told the doctor I had tested this and it would work, and he told me he was putting me back in the hospital, probably for electrotherapy.

Electrotherapy. Electric shock treatments. I recoiled. My psychiatrist and I had discussed this possibility before, and I knew he considered them a last resort for me, a kind of therapeutic sledgehammer. In the hospital, they are referred to as ECT for Electro-Convulsive Therapy, but they no longer cause convulsions, nor are they as dangerous as they once were. Nobody knows exactly what they cause or how or why they work. Whatever they do, I found them painful and unpleasant.

Thus, in February 1974, I found myself in the hospital again. I was interviewed by the electrotherapist, a psychiatrist specially trained in this field, and he agreed I might benefit from the treatments. On the morning of the first treatment, the nurse came in at six-thirty and gave me an injection of atropine to dry up bodily fluids. At seven, I was taken to the treatment room, where I lay down on a flat table. The electrotherapist, a large, genial man, smiled as if he were about to invite me to a dance and slid a needle into my arm. His assistant slid a mouthpiece into my mouth to keep me from biting my tongue, and I was given sodium pentothal, which put me to sleep in short order. The "shock" was administered at my temples, but I was aware of nothing more until I was back in my own bed.

When I woke up, I had a terrible headache; I did not know where I was or who I was; I did not recognize my roommate or my room. 1 did, however, recognize my psychiatrist, who was sitting beside the bed. I told him I would rather be dead than feel like this. I was terribly thirsty and was given a glass of water and some codeine for my headache and went back to sleep. When I reawakened, it was about eleven-thirty and I felt better —more in focus.

My reaction was not quite as bad to subsequent treatments (they were given three times a week), but I nearly always had an intense headache and frequently slept late, which, I was told, was a good sign.

One of the side effects of electrotherapy is amnesia, the severity of which varies with each individual. No one can predict how long the amnesia will last or how extensive it will be, nor can anyone say whether or not it is related to emotional factors. In my case, it was not too much of a problem and to a large extent has faded.

After eight electrotherapy treatments, I was given permission to spend the week-end at home. My psychiatrist tells me we made an explicit agreement before I went home that I would not attempt to commit suicide, but I did not then (nor do I now) remember any such agreement, and I proceeded to execute the plan I had outlined earlier.

My son had a friend over to spend the night, and they were sleeping in the guest room which is quite near the garage, but the master bedroom, where Dave was sleeping, is on the other side of the house. At about twelve-thirty that night, I attached the vacuum cleaner hose to the exhaust pipe and ran it, with one wand attached, through the rear window, lowered just far enough to accommodate it, into the car. Then I turned on the motor and climbed into the back seat with half a bottle of wine and some rum. I sat there rather happily drinking wine while the exhaust emission burned my arm so badly that I still have a mark.

At some point, I became concerned that the boys might hear the noise of the car motor and either come and investigate or report the matter to Dave, so I drove the car out of the garage. At some point, too, the exhaust emission burned a hole in the hose, so that no more carbon monoxide was coming into the car. From the time I left the garage, my memories of that night are kaleidoscopic. I remember bright lights and a montage of faces, all of whom were extraordinarily friendly. After a while, I blacked out entirely, and when I regained consciousness, I was in my own bed at home with a horrendous headache and no idea of how I got there.

Dave tells me that he woke up at two o'clock or two-thirty and when he saw that I was not in bed, he looked for me through the house, finally discovering that the car, too, was gone. He called the psychiatrist, who told him to call the police, which he did. We live in the country, but after some time, the city police called to tell him that they had found me and were bringing me home. I was wearing only a nightgown and a robe, had no identification or driver's license, and furthermore had an open bottle of rum in the car. Why I was not arrested, I don't know, and I suspect it is the better part of wisdom not to inquire. When they delivered me, the police also delivered the car keys and registration certificate. The car was within the city limits about five miles from our house. How I avoided having an accident is another miracle.

Dave returned me to the hospital that Sunday. My psychiatrist was furious, but did not abandon me, as I was afraid he might. And I had another unsuccessful suicide atempt to add to my record. In fact, my son has commented that he doesn't mind if I try to commit suicide as long as I don't succeed. The question arises as to whether my failures are deliberate. I leave the empty bottles lying around so that the drugs I have taken can be quickly identified. I leave myself lying around so that I will be found in time to have my life saved. I telegraph my intentions so that I can be stopped. My psychiatrist tells me that people who really intend to commit suicide do so, but here we are, talking to each other. And here I am, writing a book about it.

So there must be a will to live within me, a force strong enough to defeat death at every encounter. The problem is how to resolve the ambivalence, how to make the coin come up heads. I yearn for death, as this book records, but when I try to die, I fail. And every time I fail, I say, Next time I'll succeed. I must learn to set aside the words, "Next time." I must start trying to live instead of trying to die.

To this end, I am taking Antabuse so that I can no longer drink. I occupy myself with yoga lessons, because they make my body feel good. I paint, because it is exciting to work with my new-found sense of color. I work part-time for a small, weekly newspaper, which is fun because the staff is young, enthusiastic and full of vitality. And when despair threatens my sanity, I try to cool it by finding someone to talk to, or by writing it down, or by listening to the sea. And twice a week, I see my friend, the therapist.

Some day again, perhaps I shall be able to say, "Behold, I am come home unto myself."

April, 1974

Down there
where I am digging my garden,
the soil is compact and dense
and must be encouraged
by leaf mold and humus and
earthworms
to breathe.

Down there in the old horse corral
where my garden will be,
I think as I dig
that this is my statement
for the future,
but that thought is too bold;
it frightens me.

Down there
where I am digging my garden
I hold
the soil in my hands;
it slips under my fingernails
and feels moist and cool
and I wish I were already
a part of it.

PART II
April, 1974 - April, 1975

"The central (experience) . . . is the *willingness to be*, even though the outer conditions should remain the same." WILLIAM JAMES

ABOUT TWO weeks after completing the first part of this book, I again tried to commit suicide. In one closet of my mind, I had been planning to do this all along, but I had kept the door locked on it, except for what I had put down on paper. All the time I was pretending to start a new life, I was preparing to die. I told no one of my preparations, for I knew I would be stopped, and this time I could not afford to be stopped, this time I would have to succeed.

I was filled with a pervasive hopelessness. My despair and depression were unrelieved, despite the best efforts of my therapist who, it seemed to me, was now at a loss as to how to continue my treatment. I had been given every antidepressant in the book, plus a great many other psychotropic drugs, and I was now taking an antidepressant, plus a tranquilizer on a "need" basis, plus Antabuse, and I often felt overwhelmingly sleepy or drugged. Lithium had been tried when there appeared to be some remission of my depression, but because of a variety of complications, its use had to be discontinued. If my depression never ended, how could lithium be effective?

Hospitalization was certainly not indicated; whatever repairing and restoring had been possible there had already been accomplished, and I desperately did not want to go back. To reappear in those corridors would mean admitting two failures—a failure to live and a failure to die.

Electrotherapy had made it possible for me to be somewhat more assertive, but on the whole it had left me feeling as if I had been through a shredder. I was bewildered, unable to move into the new channels which had been opened. I missed alcohol and ate huge quantities of candy, ice cream and other sweets, and frequently not much else—a diet that certainly was not contributing anything toward stability.

Physically, I was not feeling at all well. I was very tired most of the time. I spent nearly every afternoon and evening in bed and usually did not have dinner with my family; Dave did almost all of the cooking and cleaning. I would gather together whatever slim resources I could unearth in order to do what had to be done, and then I would be exhausted. I wrote frenetically, spending an hour or two each day on the book, hoping that if I could put everything into written words, I would be rid of it. Instead, I think that writing about my suicidal feelings reinforced them, boxing me in with them until they became more important, more real, more true than the alleged aim of relief. Through all this, I lost contact with my son, and he frequently declared that I was not his mother, that I was a witch pretending to be his mother. I did not know how to deal with him, and he began to have temper tantrums.

My chest became very tight, and we all thought this was just another symptom of stress. I could not breathe fully, and my yoga exercises left me depleted. When I closed my eyes, I seemed to be in a car moving backward, and I felt there was no way forward, that everything had been tried and had failed, and I would never get well. Further, I felt that my illness had gone on for such a long time that it had become tiresome, boring. Nobody cared. I wasn't worth caring about. Everybody near me would be better off without me.

When I finished the book on suicide (up to April 1974), I realized that writing it had been a failure, too. Putting everything down on paper had not helped. The exorcism had not worked. My therapist, seeing how things were going with me, had counselled me to drop it, but I had refused, as I refused so much of his advice. In that interior part of my mind which was planning suicide, I held the book to be my final contribution, my legacy to those who might be curious about what went on in the mind of a suicide. Having finished it, I had nothing else to do, no more reason for hanging around. It was "Over and Out." I would die with the manuscript in my hand, as it were, establishing its validity with my own death.

And so I saved pills and planned plans and told no one. For some time my therapist had been giving me my medication in tiny amounts. At the end of each of our semi-weekly sessions, he would count out the number of pills I needed and put them in a small brown envelope. He hated this procedure, and I think he regarded it as one of the real sacrifices he made in my interest.

I took those pills exactly as directed, for I was afraid that if I cheated, he would somehow detect it. In this respect, I ascribed to him the omniscience of my mother, who had convinced me at an early age that she knew when I lied or did anything else that went against her principles, whether she had evidence of it or not. The night I lost my virginity (at age nineteen), she saw the stains on my petticoat and became so enraged that she beat me with my father's leather belt. I wonder sometimes if children should not be allowed to tell a lie occasionally and get away with it, just as a kind of insurance of their sense of privacy.

In addition to my therapist, however, I had another doctor. He knew about my suicidal history and was very supportive and sympathetic; whenever I turned up in a hospital, he was in attendance (until the last time, when he could not be present).

He treated me for arthritis, gout, bleeding hemorrhoids—and headaches. At one time, he had given me a prescription for Fiorinal, and although it was for a small quantity and was supposedly not refillable, my pharmacist refilled it for me on request without asking any questions. Thus, I had saved an attractive quantity of these pills against the day when I would need them to resolve the ultimate headache. They were tucked away, a secret cache, which, like my plan for suicide, was sometimes even hidden from myself.

And so the day came. Why did I pick that day? I don't really know. Everything had come together. The book was finished, the struggle was hopeless, and I was empty. On the previous day, I had gone to see my medical doctor about a kidney infection, and although he did everything possible, I came away with the feeling that he didn't care. On that day, too, I had seen my therapist, and, as he had failed to do something I expected him to do, I felt that he didn't care either. On the morning of the day in question, Dave and I had seen our family therapists and I felt they were far more concerned about Dave than they were about me. It was a dead end.

All of this was unreasonable, of course, but reason had nothing to do with it. I think it is rare, in our culture and at this period in our history, for suicide or attempted suicide to be a reasonable event. There are cases when the ravages of terminal illness might make suicide a logical and justifiable decision, but for most of us, the attempt to take one's life is a message of quite another sort. In my case, it said: "I am rotten and useless. Nobody can love me, nobody does love me, therefore I must die."

I was permeated with a profound sense of degradation, of helplessness and hopelessness, of being boxed into a situation from which there was no exit. My life was a trap, and I was running around inside it in meaningless patterns that didn't go anywhere or produce anything, and all around me was the twilight of despair that grew ever deeper and thicker, with not even the suggestion of a promise that there could ever be a dawn.

I was also afflicted by a kind of psychological tunnel vision that would let me see only what I wanted to see. I knew that people around me were trying, with a desperation equal to mine, to open doors for me. They were handing me keys, giving me shovels for digging, ropes for climbing, candles for seeing. But I would not accept any of these tools. I felt that my life contained only events, not purposes, and everything that people were trying to do for me was essentially irrelevant.

First, I slashed my wrist with a razor blade. Although razor blades had been taken away from me long before, I had found one in my sewing box and hidden it under a book on my bedside table. At about eleven o'clock in the morning, after Dave and I returned from our family therapy session at the hospital, I went upstairs, got the razor blade, went into the bathroom and started hacking away.

It is a picture that I will never be able to wash out of my mind, a scene of horror and revulsion, and I see it in slow motion. I leaned over the sink, moaning and crying and gasping —deep, rasping, hysterical sounds coming from an ugly well of self-hatred within me. I attacked the veins in my wrist with the razor blade wildly and recklessly, and the blood rose in great blobs and fell in sickening clots into the sink; it didn't trickle or run down the drain, it just accumulated in a thick pool like jello, and it seemed almost as unreal. The cuts hurt, but I rejoiced in the hurt, forcing myself to go on, and all the time those terrible sounds erupted from my body. Yet I never struck anything hard or deep enough to do any serious damage. Opening a blood vessel and bleeding to death is supposed to be such an easy thing to do, but I couldn't do it.

I don't think suicide was clearly in my mind at that point. What I was doing was having a temper tantrum. With every stroke of the razor, I expressed a wave of despair and grief and anger. Up came the rage and down went the razor blade. I could not live the way I was living, and I was powerless to change it. All the love I had once had was gone, and I was a shell, purposeless and unperceived. And I was angry—angry that my life held no meaning, angry that no one could give me any answers, angry at being nothing and being unable to act.

But I was grieving, too—that's what the sounds were all about—grieving for the losses of my life, the lack of purpose, the lack of love, the lack of any sense of being. They were the sounds of total despair—shuddering, sobbing, black. I felt driven into this scene, and I mourned my own action. I was the judge, I was the criminal, I was the victim. In the end, I had also to be the executioner.

Demonstrations of anger had always been forbidden in my family, and any feelings of anger or resentment toward my parents were quickly suppressed. On the other hand, my mother and father quarreled violently and often; Mother smashed the china, and Daddy radiated rage. He was a big man and frightenwhen he was angry, whether he did anything about it or not.

Thus, when I was a child, when my anger came, it was put down, shoved under the rug, forbidden. Now I was angry and I let go, let it burn, let it destroy. I was angry at my therapist, angry at my husband, angry at my son. But I could not attack any of these things, so I attacked myself. I was insane, out of control and not wanting control. My rage and grief enveloped me like a flame.

Dave heard the noises I was making and came to me. He took the razor blade out of my hand very gently and led me downstairs to my chair. I put some kleenex over the wound, which continued to bleed slowly. It was not deep, but it was about a quarter of an inch wide and an inch long. Tears ran down my cheeks, but inside I was immensely calm and remote. All the turbulence in me was stilled, and I was merely waiting to see what would happen next. I would not die from this wound, but neither would I go on living as I had been. I stared out at a world with which I no longer had any intimate relationship; I might have been a distant cousin, or the resident of some far planet brought here by accident, singularly detached and uninvolved, a spectator. I did not know it then, but I had already crossed over into the realm of death.

Dave was gravely distressed, almost frantic, and he did not know what to do. The wound was clearly not life-threatening, but it was nasty. More important was my total condition. I had done what I had promised not to do. I had seemed to be getting better, busy with things I apparently enjoyed; yet I had done this ugly thing.

He paced the floor, rubbing his hands together, holding his forehead, trying to see what could be done for me that had not already been tried. "What shall I do? What can I do? I don't know what to do," he said over and over, and I watched him from that remote place to which I had retired and wondered why he did not take me to the hospital to have the cuts sewn up. I felt great contempt for what I saw as his ineffectuality, his inability to solve my problem, and I lost interest in him.

As I watched, I realized that this was the day on which I would commit suicide. In making this mess of my wrist, I had done the ultimately unforgivable, had snuffed out whatever sympathy anyone might still have for me. I could not have had a greater sense of revulsion had I committed murder. Thus, there was only one way for me to go, and that was out. It seemed beautifully inevitable, and I was as serene about it as some women are when pregnant. I had the pills; all I needed now was the opportunity to take them. Like the impulsive murderer who suddenly sees what he has done, I looked at my wrist and knew I could not be forgiven. This was it, and this time I would not fail. I was calm, very calm. All of my emotions had been spent in the razor blade attack, and I was all intellect, coolly calculating how soon I might get on with what had to be done.

I started moving around the house, but Dave followed me wherever I went and I could not get to the place where I had hidden the pills. Finally, at about one o'clock, the postman came to the door, and while Dave was dealing with him, I went out to the kitchen. The Fiorinal was in a cupboard behind some mixing bowls, and I poured the pills into a large bottle containing about 200 aspirin tablets, adding other bits and pieces of potentially dangerous medication which we no longer used but still kept on hand. I put all of the pills into one bottle because I did not want to be caught with a lot of bottles in my hand. Just as I slipped the aspirin bottle into my pocket, Dave came into the kitchen and asked me what I was doing. "Getting some aspirin for a headache," I said.

Then I went upstairs to the bedroom, saying that I was tired and wanted to lie down, a not unusual pattern of behavior for me at that time. Therefore, Dave did not come with me. I was afraid, however, that he might come upstairs at any moment to check on me, and so I proceeded with the business at hand very quietly. I had only a tiny paper cup to put water in, and I had to refill it a great many times in order to swallow all of the pills. There were about fifty Fiorinal tablets in the top of the bottle, and I took those first. Then I took the other pills and started on the aspirin. I felt that the aspirin was a kind of insurance, the icing on the cake if you will, and I think I swallowed about a hundred of them. I stopped only because I began to feel sick and I was afraid I might throw up and spoil the whole thing. Then I lay down on the bed. I was not a writer of suicide notes. If I had been, mine would have said: "Don't forget to feed the cats."

I really believed I would die. I thought about Dave and I thought about our son, but they were remote figures. I knew they would grieve, but I knew, too, that they would recover from their grief, and I felt they would go on to better things and be happier people because they no longer had to carry me along as some sort of sick luggage. Quietly in my thoughts, I said Good-bye to both of them. I also said Good-bye to my therapist, with a deep sense of sadness and regret that I could not travel along the road he had so optimistically shown me. And that is the last thing I remember doing.

At two-thirty in the afternoon, we had to drive about two

miles down the road to meet our son's school bus. Dave usually did this chore, but on this day, he insisted that I come with him. I was still holding a bloody kleenex over my wrist, but, other than that, I must have appeared normal. After picking up our son, Dave drove to the emergency room of the hospital to have my wound stitched up. My therapist was informed from the hospital, but I was not kept there and Dave brought me home.

When we got home, I went upstairs to lie down again. Dave says I stumbled a few times and he had to help me up the stairs, but he attributed this to shock and fatigue. It was not until about seven o'clock that evening that he became suspicious, and he and our son checked on me. By then, of course, I was completely unconscious, curled up on the bed, covered with sweat. Dave called the ambulance, called the therapist saying, "She's done it again," and called up whatever reserves he had to deal with his agony.

I had plenty of time to die—about six hours from the time I took the pills until Dave called the ambulance. I should have been dead when he came upstairs to check on me. But I wasn't. Why didn't I die when I wanted to so much? Was there something absent from my desire, some inner reserve that would not let me go all the way, that would not let me achieve the final orgasm of death? I swallowed over 160 pills, and a much smaller quantity of the principal drug involved had given rise to suspicions of brain damage a year earlier. The thought crossed my mind that, if I survived, it would be with a permanently damaged brain, and who would want to live like that?

No, death was my desire. I put my very best effort into achieving it. It had been a conscious, sober decision. No booze was involved, and by the time I took the pills, my anger and grief had subsided. My insanity, if that's what it was, was of a different variety. I felt I had no right to live, but I did have a right to die. There was no other way to go.

So I tried to die and I failed. I thought that death was optional, but I was wrong.

If people who try to commit suicide are people who want to control everything, that description fits me. I was never fired from a job, I always resigned. With one exception, every love affair I had was terminated by me. I could not share responsibility. On the other hand, when I found I could not control things completely, I gave up and would have nothing to do with them. If I could not be omnipotent, then I would be powerless. But even in my impotence, I wanted control, so I tried to show I could control my life by dying.

There were a lot of "ifs" in that afternoon that profoundly affected the subsequent course of events. If Dave had taken me to the hospital immediately after I slashed my wrist, would I have taken the pills anyway? If, after he did take me to the hospital someone there had recognized the strangeness of my behavior (and I find it hard to believe that a person can walk around literally half-asleep and not betray that condition in some way) and had kept me there, that would have changed significantly the treatment I received later. The tightness in my chest turned out to be caused not by stress but by pneumonia, and if that had been diagnosed earlier, what would have happened?

And that is not the end of the "ifs." I have never before been so struck by the role chance plays in our lives. But is it chance? If I had not tried so hard to die, would I have realized how important it is to live? I had tried and failed to die before, but this was the first time I had put so much conscious effort into the attempt.

What happened next was perhaps the most fateful "if" of all. Our Sheriff's department routinely sent a deputy to accompany every ambulance. When ambulance and deputy arrived at our house, Dave told them I had taken an overdose of something, he didn't know what, and asked them to take me to the same hospital where I had so often been a patient. The deputy asked about the bandage on my wrist and, when he heard the explanation, said, "Twice in one day is too much. We'll take her to the county hospital on a 72-hour hold."

Thus began my encounter with the county hospital, a gray group of structures rambling across the landscape chronologically as well as geographically. It has all of the tubes and wires and other paraphernalia required to maintain and repair the seriously ill, but it offers no nutrition for the soul. In my memory, it is as gray and grim on the inside as it is on the outside, and for a long time it appeared in my dreams under the heading: Prison. I lived in it for two weeks—weeks that were longer than ordinary weeks because they contained not minutes and hours but nightmares. There were nightmares one after another, one on top of the other, over and under me, around me and in me. I was in them and they were my world.

For two days I was completely unconscious in the Intensive Care Unit. Then I was moved to the psychiatric ward, of which my recollections are vague and uncertain. Someone asked me the day and the date, but all I could remember was that it was April. I knew it was April and that I was happy about it, but I don't think I could articulate this knowledge. The same person asked if I could remember his name. I knew that I should be able to remember his name, but I could not bring his face into focus. Syllables of names and faces crept around in my clouded mind, but I could not bring one out into the daylight. On another occasion, I threw a thermometer at a nurse because she expressed contempt for my having put myself in this position. Someone cheered, I think.

I also remember being tied into a wheelchair so that X-ray pictures could be taken of my chest. I tried very hard to sit up straight but was completely unable to do so and kept sliding down into the chair or over the side. These X-rays revealed my pneumonia, and I was forthwith moved from the psychiatric unit to the medical floor. There, the doctors and nurses were trained in strictly medical techniques, and I did not see a psychatrist again for a week. If I found it hard to die, some old ideas find it even harder, and the superstition that the mind and the body are separate entities deserves an early execution.

This attitude meant that no one was available to me to talk about the events going on in my mind or the intense feelings I was having. Nurses recorded my vital signs, checked the catheter, replaced supplies of intravenous medication. Staff doctors came to call every morning, but they never talked to me, they talked only to each other as if I weren't there—and in a sense I wasn't. Periodically, I was bundled into a wheelchair and carted off to be X-rayed, a 5'7" rag doll.

To me, my physical condition was irrelevant. My life was going on somewhere else. Because of the drug overdose, the fever associated with the pneumonia, and the pneumonia itself, my slow and difficult return to consciousness was a haunted and hallucinated one. I was caught in some weird world of the mind which projected scenes and events around me that did not exist but were very real. If you have ever wondered which is reality —the world you experience when you are awake or the one you know when you dream—this was a beautiful example of that ambiguity.

My hallucinated life, which included an entirely non-existent time sequence, contained great vitality, warmth, color, precision and cheer, but those fixures of my environment which anyone else would have called real—the beds, the curtains, the walls, the people—were fuzzy and wobbly and cold and gray. They faded in and out of focus, indefinite and abstract, looming up in front of me and then sliding away. Space had no meaning. The wall might be near or distant, according to some rationale of its own, and wherever it was, it never looked very solid. I could have put my foot through it as if it were a cloud. My own body, when I was aware of it at all, had an equal lack of substance.

When I was a child, I frequently had high fevers as a result of tonsillitis. They were always accompanied by a feeling that the world was made of soggy bread—a very sick, thick kind of bread that coated my tongue with some sort of gray substance I could not get rid of. During those first few days in the medical ward, the county hospital was made of soggy bread, furry and moldy and insubstantial.

"Soon I will wake up," I thought, "and I will be home and everything will be all right." Neither of the worlds I perceived could be the real one. The furniture could not be real because it was too fuzzy and insecure. But the sharply-defined motion pictures I saw everywhere could also not be real because they were too fantastic. There must be some other reality somewhere. I would wake up at any moment into the real, real world in which I lived. I struggled toward this awakening through the colorless, opaque curtains hanging in front of my eyes and thickening my tongue and my mind.

Then one day Dave came to see me, and when I saw him there beside the bed and knew that he at least was real, inside my hallucinated world and sitting on one of those chairs that I could not quite bring into focus, I realized I would not wake up and find myself at home, safe and comfortable.

It was then I knew I was really here, in this place, in this bed, into which I was locked with a belt that fastened around my waist and tied me to the mattress. I knew I was going to have to come to terms with that fact, motion pictures to the contrary notwithstanding. That instant of focus on Dave's presence beside the bed was truly awesome. I think it was the first time I realized I was alive. He was here and I was here and life was inescapable. "I wish I had succeeded," I said. Poor, grieving man. How could I be so cruel?

This was when my curious misapprehension of time occurred. It seemed to me Dave said our son was going to have a week's vacation from school and that, because the hospital did not allow children to visit patients, he would not be able to come and see me. I was too confused to remember that the school schedule included no such week's vacation. Later, when I thought about it, I felt that Dave's failure to visit me during this "week" betrayed a final erosion of his feeling for me. I had tried to commit suicide once too often and he could no longer tolerate it and was therefore unwilling to make whatever arrangements were necessary for him to come to the hospital alone.

Between Dave's visit on Friday and his next visit on the following Monday, a whole week went by for me, a very real week, full of events, nurses, doctors, sounds, and sights, including all that bewildering magnificence on the wall. Prominent in this apparent week was the old woman who occupied the bed next to mine. She was senile and vicious, with one arm in a long bandage which she was always trying to unravel. She would tease me until I cried, and then she would tease me about crying. She would pull back the curtain separating our beds and say, "Lady." If I tried to ignore her, the soft voice saying, "Lady, Lady," wove itself insidiously into my thoughts until I had to look at her. As soon as she had my attention, she would do something destructive, such as remove the intravenous needle from her arm, knowing that I would ring for the nurse. She tormented me unmercifully, and I gradually identified with her. She was sick and I was sick, and we were together in our insanity. "You're no better than I am," she would say, and I knew she was right.

This woman actually existed, for I saw her again before I left the hospital, but whether all of our encounters really took place, I don't know. She was Russian, and so became for me a replica of my crazy grandmother, except that she was more talkative and vindictive. In her later years, my grandmother lost track of names and always addressed me as "Lady," as if she had long ago forsworn our relationship. The woman in the hospital repeatedly asked my name and then refused to acknowledge that she knew it. She tormented me day and night, until finally, in a moment of lucidity, I told a nurse I could no longer be responsible for her. She was then moved to another room, and I can only be grateful to the staff for perceiving my distress—that is, if these things really happened.

I heard many conversations up and down the hall and in

other rooms of the hospital with remarkable clarity. Some of them, I know, did not take place, but about others I am not so sure. One night, for example, a woman was brought in and placed in the room next to mine. I heard her say distinctly that she had murdered her husband and had then been raped by about ten men. "I guess I'm a murderer," she said, and then giggled coyly. Laughing happily, she talked to someone about these events the entire night and well into the next day. But that night and day didn't exist. Did she?

I gave a great many parties, wore beautiful garments, and entertained beautiful people. I lived in a great many different houses, all imaginatively designed and decorated, with red tile roofs, flagstone patios, oriental rugs. I sang a lot, sad songs like "The Wild Goose Grasses." I remember once being all curled up and humming; the nurse grew angry when she saw me, for I was lying on the I.V. tube, cutting off the flow of medication into my body. Also, I cried. One day, a nurse asked me why I was crying and I said it was because I wanted to be loved. "Please," I begged, "won't somebody love me?" I thought that if someone would just hold me, cuddle me like an infant, I would be all right. It did not seem such a big request, but the nurse went away.

I was very lonely and bewildered and didn't understand anything going on around me. Sometimes I perceived the hospital room as in a flash of lightning. It would be illuminated briefly and then would fade away. People I did not know appeared and disappeared, regarding me with the cool detachment of the medical profession, observing me, listening to my sounds.

As my periods of true consciousness lengthened, I realized that the nurses were giving me aspirin to bring down my fever. Considering how much aspirin was already in my system, this was not contributing to my recovery of a sense of reality, and I refused to take any more. On another occasion, I had a violent headache, so severe that I could not move, but I would not accept an analgesic for it because I was afraid to take any more drugs. The pain, no matter how intense, was preferable to the world of hallucination.

Somewhere during the course of that non-existent week, I hit bottom. I, who had previously sneered at such an idea. Helpless on the bed, fever-ridden, spitting blood, unable to breathe cleanly, I was a dreg, a bit of muck, primordial matter tossing at the bottom of the sea. My hallucinatory world, although it was pretty and colorful and full of song, was a world of madness, an underwater world consisting of distortions and uncertainties. In that undersea world, nothing was predictable, and I wanted, more than anything, to get my head out of the water, to see clearly again. The idea that I might be permanently trapped down there, unable to perceive anything correctly and forever groping for the surface, terrified me. If I stayed, I would drown, and would have to make the massive adjustment required of a madman, an adjustment to a world governed by no discernible rules and forever devoid of the possibility of peace, love and growth.

I could have stayed mad, I guess, fumbling along, with my distortions, my obsessions, my sickness, there at the bottom of the sea. The dreg could have remained a dreg, drifting along into death. But, for reasons I hardly understand, the dreg decided to grow, decided to become.

On that hospital bed, with my physical impotence almost complete and with my mind going in and out of focus like a faulty slide projector, I decided against dreg-ness. I can't cite day and hour, I can't describe it as some dramatic achievement of enlightenment or revelation, I can't declare that suddenly everything was clear, because it wasn't like that. All I can say is that, somewhere, somehow, deep down in my being, I changed course.

It was a very quiet, very interior thing, and not a process of awareness at all. It just seemed to come about. Perhaps all of the truly major events of our lives occur just as subtly: falling in love, getting pregnant, selecting a career. The pressures are there, pushing and pulling all the time; the influences arising from our genetic and environmental inheritance move us this way and that; our desires and dreams, our fears and aspirations, all the fibers wound together in the enormously complicated and ingeniously assembled structure of the human mind come together from time to time to show us the way, illuminate the road.

In just such a strange and subtle way, during a week that didn't exist, I altered my direction. Not all at once, and not very dramatically. In fact, I wasn't fully aware of the change until much later. All I knew at the time was that I wanted to go home. I was impatient with the hospital, impatient with the doctors and the nurses and the endless accumulation of hours spent in bed, and I wanted out of there. I wanted to go home where I felt I could grow, and maybe even blossom. It seemed a simple thing, but it turned out not to be simple at all. Why couldn't I just get out of bed and go home? Lots of reasons.

First of all, I was still sick. Even after the hallucinations stopped, I had pneumonia to contend with, and that did not clear up for another week.

Then there was the question of after-care. I had been admitted on a 72-hour psychiatric hold, and although I had been in the hospital considerably longer, I had spent very little time in the psychiatric unit. Therefore, when I was released by the medical doctors, I would still be referred back to the hospital psychiatrist. When the psychiatrist finally saw me, he told me he would not authorize my discharge until he was assured I would have adequate after-care. This meant that if I were not released into the care of my own psychiatrist, I would be held in the psychiatric unit until other arrangements could be made. On both counts, I would have to stay.

I desperately wanted to avoid a return to the psychiatric unit. I remembered the nurse at whom I had thrown the thermometer and wondered if all of the nurses were like that. I was afraid to go back there, lest she still feel hostile toward me, for I knew that a nurse could make life miserable for a patient in many ways. What if there were other nurses who felt as she did?

Moreover, I felt more strongly than ever that my place now was at home, and the sooner I got there, the better. It was only there that I could begin picking up the pieces and putting them back in place; it was only there that I could reconstruct a useful world for myself. Home had become the only place where I could be restored, where my life could be confirmed, because it was real and the hospital environment was not. I could no longer solve my problems by being protected from them. The time for that was gone, and I wanted to go home where my problems were. I was ready to live.

So I considered how I was to get home. And it was here that I became painfully aware of the absence of my therapist. As a patient in the county hospital, I was not directly in his care. By putting me in a county facility, the sheriff had made me a matter of public, rather than strictly private, concern, and I had not seen my therapist since my arrival at the hospital.

But his absence had greater significance. By trying once again to commit suicide, I had been defying him and everything he had done or tried to do for me. I had been saying, "Fuck you," in the most violent and terrible way I could think of. He had told me that this was what I was doing, but I did not believe him. I could not believe him. How could my self-destructive actions be directed toward him, whom I admired, respected and loved? How could I harbor such virulent hostility toward someone who had been both father and mother to me, someone who had shown me seemingly infinite compassion and understanding and had always been there, holding out his hand, when I tried to die? I could not accept that, I could not believe it, it wasn't true. I even asked one of the nurses to send him a message to tell him that it wasn't true.

But it was true. A hard, hard truth, bitter and cold and unavoidable. A truth that every child knows and then forgets. For the reason it was true lay in the very fact that he had, in my eyes, been both father and mother to me, and I had endowed him with all of their imagined power, as well as other more realistic qualities, as part of the phenomenon called transference. I expected miracles of intuition and skill from him, but I also did not really believe that he cared. Thus, I invested him with enormous power, on the one hand, which he could use or not as he saw fit, and, on the other, I felt that he was not using this power for my benefit, that he was denying me, neglecting me. According to this view, he could have cured me if he really wanted to, and the fact that he did not cure me meant both that he didn't care and that I wasn't worth caring about.

Consequently, I was hurt, and I was angry, but these feelings were too intense for me to acknowledge. I shoved them under the rug, where they bubbled and boiled along with all the old, long-suppressed feelings I had had toward my real parents and never dared to express. Children frequently hate their parents and today, at least, they are permitted to say so. I could not have said so. On the occasions when I hated my mother, I stamped out the feeling so ruthlessly that it ceased to exist anywhere close to the conscious level. I could not say I hated her because I did not feel hatred. I could not feel hatred because I would not let myself feel it. It was far, far too dangerous. This was the real reason for the intense hostility I felt toward Dave when I took LSD—I had identified him not with my father but with my mother. It was the reason for the painful anger I felt toward my therapist, anger which I could not acknowledge. So my feelings bubbled there under the rug and finally erupted in another, far more destructive way.

When my mind began emerging from its disorder, I realized only that my therapist was not there and had not been there, and I did not know what to do. At first, I felt lost. I did not have access to a telephone, but I sent messages to him by way of my husband and was told that he had been in touch with the staff psychiatrist at the hospital. When I talked with the staff psychiatrist, he suggested that my therapist might very well decide he could no longer be helpful to me, that we had reached the end of the string, and that further atempts at therapy would be self-defeating, even dangerous. In that event, he said, he would assist me in arranging for some other kind of after-care, either with the hospital outpatient department or with another therapist.

I became alarmed. Going to another therapist meant reestablishing all that faith and trust in someone else, and that would take time. I did not want to spend that kind of time and I did not want to make that kind of investment again. Also, I was afraid that a new therapist would mean a new transference and a re-enactment of the whole scene. I shuddered.

"Look," I said, "I'm not going to try to commit suicide any more. Tell him that. For me, suicide is no longer a viable alternative." I said these words without preparation, but as soon as they were spoken, I knew they were true. No matter what happaned, I would not, could not, go that route. I have since been told that suicide is one way of coping. Not a very good way, but a way. Well, I was going to find some other way of coping, and I felt my own therapist could help me find that way better and faster than some stranger. My problem was to convince him that I was serious.

Thus was my decision expressed in words, and thus did I come to recognize its presence. For, in a sense, it is incorrect to say that I "made" a decision; it is far more accurate to say that I became aware of one. I found my decision while looking around for a way to re-establish contact with my therapist. It had been lying there waiting for me, unperceived until I stumbled over it that morning. Then, it rose up in me like a wave cresting in the sea, having all the authority of a religious conversion. It was a conviction born somewhere deep inside of me, and it was total. My life would now be devoted to living.

Now I had a new problem. Although I knew the sincerity of my decision, I had trouble conveying it to others. How many times had people heard me say that I was sorry, that I felt like a heel, that I didn't want to do that again, that I would try harder? To the world, I still sounded like a reformed alcoholic after only one day without booze. I was the only one who knew that this was not the same superficial remorse. My position was like that of the boy who had too often cried, "Wolf." Who would believe me?

Dave believed me. At least, he tried to, probably because he needed to. He came to see me every day (having missed that mysterious week, which existed in my mind but not on the calendar), and I waited eagerly for his visits. I was keenly aware of his love for me; he brought it to me every day at the hospital as a kind of radiance which, even when he was not there, gave me strength.

I had stopped believing in love at some point. "Love," I had said, "is not enough. You are not enough. You are weak, you are like my father, you are inadequate to my needs." Now, however, I saw that Dave's strength was of a variety not often found. He was like a rock that could not be ground down. During all the months of my illness, the weeks of hospitalization, the repeated suicide attempts, the inability to function, and my obvious loss of faith in him, he remained solid, always there, his very immobility an asset. My expectations of him, like my expectations of my therapist, had been impossible of fulfillment. At the time of our marriage, Dave had been a prime mover, a do-er, an act-or, a person of enormous vitality. When he ceased being these things, I put him down as someone of no consequence, just as I put myself down as non-existent. More, I thought his loss of vitality was somehow my fault, and in hating myself for having done this to him, I also hated him for having let me do it.

Now my days centered on his visits, for he was my only link with the outside world, the world I wanted to re-enter as a full citizen. I realized his strength, and I realized his love, a love that had abided quietly, waiting for me to get well, always holding onto the belief that I would get well. Dave's love was the kind that gives the beloved freedom. He never put a fence around me, never tried to make my decisions for me, always let me follow whatever path I chose. When I was sick, I misinterpreted this as care-lessness, but it was in fact the very best kind of caring.

When I came home from the hospital, the statement, "Dave loves me," was one of the supports I clung to when the going got rough. His giving me room to find out who I was and then to be who I was, even at the risk that I might ultimately reject him, was a significant factor in my recovery.

In the beginning, Dave was the only person who believed me. Others were skeptical. My son, for example, when I finally saw him and told him I would no longer try to commit suicide, dismissed my assertions with: "Suicide is a household word at our house." The hospital psychiatrist said merely that such a conversion was "possible," and that the first person I had to convince was myself.

But the person I most wanted to convince was my therapist, and I had my opportunity when he came to see me at the hospital. As soon as he walked into the room, however, I saw that he was not going to be kind, receptive and accepting, willing to go along with anything I suggested. His face was grim, and his eyes regarded me without warmth. He was very much the father figure at that moment, the father to whom I had said "Fuck you" once too often, and I knew that none of my skill with words would persuade him, as it had so often persuaded others to do what I wanted them to do: the rabbi who really didn't want to convert me to Judaism, the psychiatrist who really didn't want to give me LSD, my mother who really didn't want me to leave home and go to New York.

But I talked anyway, trying to put all my hopes and fears into language, and hoping that the strength of my conviction would be communicated to him in other ways as well. I wanted not to cajole him into doing something against his will, but to convince him of my sincerity. My conversion was certain, but there were wobbles all around me. My recovery would be so much simpler and faster if it could be accomplished with his assistance, because he knew me and because I trusted him. I felt I was ready to deal with my problems as problems and not as chimeras that someone could dissolve by magic. I also needed to resolve, with him, the feelings that had surfaced because of the transference, and I felt I was ready to deal with those feelings now, within the safe context of our relationship.

He listened for about an hour, and in the end he said, "I don't know. We've been through all this before, and I don't know if I can continue to be useful to you as a therapist. After all, your life is at stake." He meant, of course, that if I continued to act out my hostility in a suicidal manner, I might very well succeed in dying. If some accidents are really suicides, some suicides are really accidents. I had been going down a path that could have only one end.

He said he would have to think about it further. This was Wednesday afternoon, and he told me he would let me know his decision by the time I was ready to be released from the medical ward. In that way, I would know whether I could go straight home or would have to return to the psychiatric unit.

I thought I would be ready to be discharged on Friday, but on Thursday, I suffered a relapse. My temperature went up, and the X-rays showed that my lungs were still congested. My white blood cell count wasn't right, either. The doctor shook his head, "You can't leave yet." "Why not?" I cried in annoyance. He smiled with that kind of forbearing patience and lack of understanding that some doctors must learn in medical school. "You're still sick," he said.

I chafed, and waited. Healing can take a long time, proceeding on several levels, which don't always move in the same direction at the same pace. Part of me was well and ready for the world, but other parts were trailing behind.

I waited all day Thursday. And all day Friday. And all day Saturday. And all day Sunday. I waited all those nights, too, for I could not sleep. The occupant of the room across the hall played his television set until eleven o'clock every night, and the sounds of the programs he watched frightened me. People are always going insane on television, or else they are dying or killing or expressing violence in some other way. Any expression of violence hurt me physically (as it would for some time), so I tried not to listen, sometimes covering my head with a pillow. Later, in the silent dark, I lisened for the sounds of a nurse's footsteps, and even welcomed the periodic arrival of a technician to record my temperature and blood pressure. I find that the worst thing about sleeplessness is silence. One feels terribly alone and vulnerable, the only person awake for miles and miles and miles. In New York, when I could not sleep, I listened to the radio; at home in California, I hear crickets and owls and mocking birds in their season, all punctuated by the occasional distant sound of a train. Maybe there should be a club for insomniacs, someone you can call and listen to and be reassured that someone else is awake, too.

The daytime was little better, except that there were more sounds in it. The nurses, though sympathetic, were much too busy for idle conversation, so I made friends with the young man who mopped the floor, a fairly articulate person who was marking time before deciding which way his life was going to go. He told me that when I was first brought to the medical ward, I slept all of the time. Sleep? So that's what it looked like.

Now and then, I was able to take a short walk, and once a student nurse untangled the threads of the I.V. equipment sufficiently to enable me to take a bath and wash my hair. Then it was discovered that I had some sort of scalp infection (which did not clear up completely for months). The hospital doctor who diagnosed it as dermatitis asked: "Is your health good?"

Food was served at prescribed intervals but was generally tasteless and unappealing. Why should I need food, I thought, when I wasn't doing anything? I ate, but eating was a chore.

The minutes passed. Time dripped slowly, and each drop was a globule of boredom and frustration. The doctors continued to shake their heads, and there was no word from my therapist.

Why was everything taking so long? Why was everyone moving so slowly? Couldn't they see, couldn't they know, that I was waiting in a hurry? "Rest while you can," someone said enviously, but this was not the kind of resting I wanted to do. I had been resting for too long, retreating for too long. The time had come to move. And the place I wanted to move to was home.

"I love you," I said to Dave one day when he came to visit me, and he wept. The fact that I could say those words confirmed the change in me more than anything else, and he knew it. I think it was then that he really began to hope again.

I got better. The tubes were detached, the belt unfastened. I walked farther and for longer periods, pushing strength back into my body. I was able to read for brief intervals. A friend had given me William James' *The Varieties of Religious Experience,* and reading it was to help, in a major way, to corroborate my new point of view toward life.

My ability to focus, however, continued to fluctuate, and I frequently felt myself slpping into some other world where I did not want to be. There were times when I held on to the side rails of the bed to reassure myself that I was not drowning. This sporadic loss of reality frightened me; I was afraid of what I might do during one of those episodes.

On Friday, I was able to get to a public telephone, and I called my therapist's office to leave a message stating that I would be willing to continue therapy without medication, thereby completely eliminating the possibility that I might misuse drugs he prescribed for me. I felt it was essential to demonstrate to him the validity of my change in direction.

By Sunday, the doctor could no longer detect signs of pneumonia in my lungs. On Monday, he said I could leave, but where I would go was up to the psychiatrists. There was no message from either of them, and I wandered around all morning trying not to think. What would I do if I had to remain in the hospital? What could I do? It seemed such a waste of time.

For the first time in two weeks, I got dressed. I was very thin, and the clothes felt strange. I sat on my bed. Snails can move pretty fast, I decided. Faster than time. Faster than psychiatrists. A nurse's aide came in. "I'm leaving today," I announced. Leaving for where, I wondered. "Oh," she replied, "we can strip your bed." I looked in the bag containing the clothes I had worn when I arrived at the hospital. They were rumpled into a ball, tired and sad, and I felt I would never wear them again because the memory they contained was almost a palpable presence.

Noon and lunch made their appearance. I ate, because time passes when you eat. Not much, but a little. It's surprising how little time eating takes, considering how important it is. I walked up and down the corridor. All around me were sick people and busy nurses. Everyone must know I did not belong here, but when would the message come? Had I been forgotten?

I went back to my room and waited, looking at the tips of my fingers, at the surface of the walls. I had spent an entire lifetime in this room, and now I was ready to leave. It had been a kind of womb, but now I needed to be born.

If the message is delivered by one of the nurses, I thought, it will mean I have to go to the psychiatric unit, but if the hospital psychiatrist delivers it in person, it will mean I am being discharged.

At two-fifteen, the psychiatrist came through the doorway, crossed the floor, and sat down on the bed next to mine. He smiled, and I knew what the message was. "You can go home. You have an appointment with your therapist tomorrow at four-thirty."

Home. I could have hugged him. Home. "Thank you," I said, and ran down the hall to the public phone. Home. I dialed the number and Dave answered. "I'll have to shave," he said. "Don't shave!" I cried. A woman sitting nearby looked up and smiled. Returning her smile, I started to cry. "I'm coming home," I wept. "I'm coming *home*. There's no time to shave."

The hospital was about fifteen miles from our house, and Dave and our son did not arrive until almost three o'clock, but this waiting was joyful. "Those were three of the longest weeks of my life," I said, as we checked out. Dave shook his head. "No, Mary, it's only been two weeks." Only two weeks? That was ridiculous. I knew I had been there for three weeks. I had counted the days, ticking them off the fingers of my impatience. "See," Dave said, pointing to the hospital record, "you came in on April 23rd, and today is the sixth of May."

Our son was excruciatingly casual. He would not let me hug him, and acted as if taking me home were a matter of small imporance. After all, why not? This had all happened before. Momma tried to commit suicide, Momma went to the hospital in an ambulance. Momma came home, contrite and apparently better. It had been going on for a year-and-a-half, and he had no reason to suppose that this time was any different. In the car, he showed me a card trick and finally put his arm around my shoulders. The touch of that arm was one of the sweetest I had ever felt. Could he dare to love me again? Could he dare to trust me? He remained aloof for some days, and he suffered from a deep unease. To him as to my husband, I had to demonstrate, morning by morning and encounter by encounter, that I was in truth a member of the family, and that I intended my presence to be permanent.

Coming home was no grand solution. On that first afternoon, I discovered that the feeling of going out of focus was not a function of the hospital environment. One minute, everything was sharp and clear and beautiful, the next it would blur and grow hazy, and I would start sliding away from here into somewhere else. It was as if reality were pulsing, but not in any predictable way, for when things drifted away from me, I could not be certain they would return. "I'm here," I would say to myself, "I'm here, I'm here, I'm here. I mustn't let go, not for a minute. Dave loves me, our son loves me, they both need me, and I am something. I'm here, I'm here, I'm here." But often I felt as if I were on a shaky suspension bridge strung out over a deep chasm; there was only a thin rope to hold onto, and the wind was blowing.

In the beginning, I could not think of the past, I could only concentrate on here and now, taking one step at a time, a new person learning to walk. As might be expected, that walking was pretty unsteady, physically as well as mentally. For weeks, my hands shook so much that I could not write legibly or hold a paint-brush, and I had to be careful when I lifted a teacup to my mouth. Working around the house, which had deteriorated terribly during my illness, I got tired now and then, but I would not lie down for any reason until bedtime.

To lie down, or even admit that I felt tired, would have been pushing everybody's panic button. Fatigue—constant fatigue, unrelenting and irremediable—had been one of the symptoms of my illness. Now, if I said, "I'm tired, I'll do that in a minute," Dave and our son looked at me in alarm. Is she getting sick again? Are we in for another repeat? I was keenly aware of their concern and took my brief rests when no one would notice. Later, when I was more secure, I protested that everyone had a right to get tired, that even metal suffers fatigue. "I get so scared," Dave said. "I don't know what I'd do if you got depressed again." He watched me carefully, and I had to be certain he knew where I was and what I was doing every minute of the day.

I was busy, and wanted to be that way—around the house, in town, here and there exploring. Doors were opening on all sides, and I wanted to look through each one of them. Oddly enough, although I was weak from the pneumonia, I had more energy than before going into the hospital. It was as if some new source of energy had become available to me, and I could now investigate more of the possibilities presented. I had always been a low-energy person, and either could not do some of the things I wanted to do because I was too tired or did them with the assistance of alcohol. This latter solution wasn't much good because, when the alcohol dissipated, the fatigue rushed back in double measure. So, I might be able to save today, but it would be at the expense of tomorrow. I thnk it entirely possible that energy formerly required to support and fight my illness was now at hand for other uses.

I began writing poetry again, with a different kind of awareness. "Today is a poem," I wrote, describing my happiness in the little things that occupy a day. When I was in focus, I could concentrate on the little things and find abundant peace and beauty in them. They were a song of joy that surrounded me, a flow of life with neither beginning nor ending. I sang a lot and cried a lot, not because I was sad or felt unloved, but because I knew myself to be a part of love and was no longer bound. I was free to choose life; I didn't need death any more.

Not that I always saw things from that bright a pinnacle—the down places were pretty low, and I was often unsure of my direction. But at least, when I lost my focus, I could remember the joy and know it existed, gradually incorporating it more and more firmly into my life.

Some of this, I suppose, was due to the residue of drugs in my system, but it also reminded me of the way I had felt after I took LSD. My experience in the hospital had all of the earmarks of a full-blown psychedelic adventure, and I was now having to repair the boundaries between conscious and unconscious, a repair that is necessary if one is to function in society. But this time, while repairing boundaries, I was going to try to understand them. I would not just put the lid on and put a stop to the whole thing. That had been necessary before, but the result was that the stuff in the pot continued to bubble and ferment until it almost destroyed me.

Often I was scared, really scared. I was afraid I would "go insane," lose control, and do something to harm myself. Thoughts of suicide tormented me. I read about a woman who jumped off a bridge, and I thought, "I could do that." When I tried to put this thought aside, it became more intense, and so I tried to deal with it in another way. I imagined myself walking across the bridge in question. I saw myself stop in the middle and look over the side into the chasm below, and then I deliberately turned and continued walking until I reached the other side. I repeated this fantasy over and over until I was sure that the next time I came to that bridge in real life, I would not be compelled to jump.

Then there was the matter of the suicide note I did not write: "Don't forget to feed the cats." We feed our two cats raw kidney. When we shop, we buy a week's supply, cut it up, and freeze it. Every afternoon, one portion must be removed from the freezer to thaw in time for the cats' dinner. This was a task I usually remembered and Dave usually forgot. Thus, when I was getting ready to die, I was concerned that the meat would not be taken out of the freezer, and the cats would starve. You may think this shows a strange sense of proportion, but suicidal thinking is not especially noted for its clarity.

At any rate, I wanted to remind my family to feed the cats when I was no longer around, and this thought came back to haunt me during the weeks following my return from the county hospital. If I neglected to take the cat food out of the freezer in time for their dinner, I became alarmed. Did that mean some underground current in my mind was moving toward suicide again? Did that mean thoughts of suicide were still alive and well somewhere?

My manuscript on suicide lay beside my typewriter, but I would not look at it, could not look at it. I was afraid that if I read it, I might get caught in that kind of thinking again. I wondered if I would ever be able to look at it or tolerate exposure to negative thinking again. When I mentioned it to people who were interested in my welfare, they all gently suggested I forget it. Perhaps, I thought, I would always have to live with a wary eye toward the beginning of a dark thought, much as the alcoholic lives with a constant prohibition of that first drink.

When I lay awake at night, tortured by fear and questioning whether I would ever come all the way up out of the water, whether I would ever feel solid inside myself again, I drew strength from the knowledge that I had no suicide plan. In the past, I had always had suicide as an ultimate recourse, frequently harboring a specific plan to use at a moment's notice. Now, although suicidal thoughts occurred to me, they were not backed up by methods and procedures. I had no plan to die, and in a curious way this set me free to live.

In those early months, I often had the feeling that the path in front of me constantly forked, that every waking moment required a new choice. One road led to stability and self-acceptance, the other to disorder and death. And my choice could not be taken for granted; it required relentless vigilance. "I can go either way with this," I said one day to the therapist, "and I don't know which way to go." "Yes you do," he replied. And when I consulted myself, I found he was right; I did know.

There are times, however, when consulting yourself doesn't seem to work, because you are in unfamiliar territory and don't recognize the signs. I had a tendency to repeat past mistakes, bad habits of thought which had accrued over such a long period that I did not know they were there. My therapist came down hard on me when he saw that I was slipping into those old patterns. For example, I had to have things be a certain way, regardless of the facts. Always, I had refused to accept some of the circumstances of my life, such as Dave's illness, insisting that they did not exist. If you order black coffee in a restaurant and the waitress puts sugar in it, there are several things you can do. You can drink it anyway, you can send it back and ask for another cup of coffee, or you can walk away from it. I refused to do any of those things. I insisted that somebody, somehow, take the sugar out of the coffee. The fact that it could not be done was irrelevant. If it were not done, I would kill myself.

Up to a point, such behavior might be called willfulness, the attitude of a child who will have a bicycle for his birthday, no matter how often it is explained that there is no money for the bicycle. In my case, the determination became obsessive: I would have Dave be as he was when I married him—exactly that and no other way. I would not leave him, I would not adjust to the change in him, I would not consider any alternative, or even admit that an alternative existed. I was obsessed with the fantasy that he could be as he had been, and no evidence to the contrary was acceptable.

This kind of thinking was carried to its logical conclusion in my obsession with suicide. While I was suicidal, any suggestion that I could get better or that there were alternatives was almost automatically transformed into a reason for killing myself. The road I walked went only one way, and signs pointing out roads going in other directions were not only ignored, they were not even seen.

Thus, obsessive thinking about one thing could lead to obsessive thinking about another and far more dangerous ambition, and had to be stopped. Okay, you say, don't think that way any more. Simple? Not simple. Not at all. First, you have to identify such a thought pattern, and that is perhaps the hardest part. We learn to think much as we learn to walk. At first, we are keenly aware of every tiny muscle that must be engaged and mobilized to produce the desired result, but as soon as the whole thing has been accomplished and coordinated, we refer it to some automatic monitoring system which thenceforth handles the entire operation. If, in this learning process, an error creeps in, throwing us slightly off balance or contributing an element of awkwardness to our gait, that too will be incorporated more or less permanently unless something radical happens to force us to change it. You walk as you walk, but if you were asked to specify the muscles involved, you would be unable to do so.

Thinking patterns are equally difficult to identify, to isolate and examine. Moreover, we do not want to examine them, much less change them. They belong to us, like that old, comfortable chair we have been sitting in for so many years that it is molded to our contours. The trouble for me was that the chair I had been using had thrown my body out of alignment.

Learning is tough. It requires stretching, it requires revising, and, in some cases, it requires surgery. It hurts. It hurts hard.

Some of the lessons I had to learn bit into me like acid, and I felt strung out, thin and fragile. I'll break, I thought, I'll surely break. But when I tried to turn away from the lessons, when I tried to reject my own truths, the hurt was worse, the threat of breaking more real.

And so, kicking and screaming, I learned—learned to spot the obsessive pattern, chop it up and divert it, whether it was about jumping off a bridge or how to get the sink unplugged. At one point, I even found that I was thinking obsessively about thinking obsessively.

I also learned that no one was going to take care of me. Mother, in the person of my therapist, was not going to take me in her arms and cuddle me, protecting me from danger. "I want to be loved," I had told the nurse, meaning that I wanted to be cradled, crooned over, and made well. I had thought by some magic my therapist could do this, because, after all, wasn't he the ideal combination: mother/father/doctor/God? I said as much one bright June day when I sat in his office. He shook his head, saying gently, "That's not my function."

Not take care of me? The recognition of this simple fact was brutal. If he didn't, who would? Who could? If no one took care of me, I would perish, sliding back down that road into despair. Stunned, I left his office and drove over to my son's school to wait for him. Arriving early, I sat in the car, trembling and clutching the steering wheel. The trees were newly green and I counted the leaves; a mocking bird was singing and I listened intently, trying to memorize the notes. No one was going to take care of me. The therapist was not my mother, and my mother was dead. The sun shone on the leaves, on the windshield, on the song of the mocking bird, but it did not shine on me. I was sick and alone and no one was going to take care of me. Afraid I would not survive that knowledge, I could only hang onto the steering wheel.

Then my son got into the car. "Hi, Mom. What's the matter?" I looked at him and touched his cheek. I was not alone, and I was no longer sick. My mother was all dreadfully dead, and my therapist was not my mother. I was free to take care of myself. "I'm okay," I said.

When I was a child, my mother took my feelings away from me. That sounds impossible, but it isn't. She did it, first, by identifying my feelings for me before I had a chance to identify them for myself. "You're angry," she would say accusingly. "No, I'm not," I would reply, and to prove it I would stifle my anger just to demonstrate that she was wrong. This led to confusion in identifying real feelings. She also tried to protect me from my feelings, saying such things as: "I wish I could feel your hurt for you, so that you wouldn't have to feel it." This sounds compassionate, but in effect it deprived me not only of my pain but also of my right to pain. I grew up with the idea that my pain wasn't real, that she (or someone else) could magically feel my pain for me, so that I could move along comfortably insulated from it.

Thus, I had to re-learn my feelings, and in the process discover that my pain was my own, that there was no one anywhere who could bear it for me. Pain, I found, is necessary for growth.

Growing is not a steady progression from here to there, occurring as neatly as a highway from one town to the next; it is a matter of chunks and hunks which often accrue underground and then burst forth to show us what we have learned. The process also involves waste and discard and separation and therefore hurts. My separation from my mother when I first went away to college had been disastrous. I now faced a different kind of separation: the necessary separation of mother and son. Although my son was not about to leave home, he was struggling to establish personal independence, and I had to learn to let him do that. In the past, when I had said, "Okay, do it your way," I had meant, "Okay, do it your way as long as you end up doing it my way."

The first step I had to take was to realize I didn't have to take one. "Creative nonintervention," my therapist called it. I didn't even have to say, "Okay, do it your way." All I had to do was let him do it his way and be on hand if his way didn't work out. Or congratulate him if it did.

That required recognizing him as a separate person, with thoughts, feelings, plans and experiences all his own. This was surprisingly difficult. I knew intellectually what I had to do, but confirming it emotionally was another matter. I did not want to let go of him. I wanted to keep him close under my heart, as if he were still in my womb and I had a right to know his private life because it was fed by me. He was born by Caesarean Section, as my body was not preparing itself for natural childbirth when it was due, and I wonder if, even then, I was refusing to let him go.

The separation was essential, however, no matter how much it hurt. It was like having my skin peeled off, layer by layer, but I gained something far more valuable than what I thought I was losing. I gained love, and I gained respect. In accepting my son as a separate person, no longer bound to me, I affirmed not only his individuality, but also my own. It was another step in learning my freedom to be.

I observed many "anniversaries." Every day of survival was a triumph. I could say, Look at that! Four days, five days, six days out of the hospital. Then it was weeks. And finally months. These observations marked not only time but progress, for although I could not see my recovery in the transition from one day to the next, I could see it when I compared this week with two weeks ago. My ups were more consistent; my downs did not dip so low; my focus was maintained for longer and longer periods.

In August, we went back to Colorado, where I visited my father, finding I had lost much of my previous rancor toward him and could regard him as a person apart from whatever role he had played as my father. I could feel compassion for the problems he faced and enjoy his recollections. It was a tremendous experience and contributed greatly to my sense of being liberated from the past while simultaneously being able to assimilate it.

The experience had its negative aspect as well. While we were there, I decided to cook a meal for my father—and burned my hand severely on hot grease. Although I put my hand in cool water immediately, we finally had to go to the local hospital for treatment. As the doctor inspected my hand, tears were streaming down my face. Thinking they expressed pain, he offered me some codeine, but I was not crying because my hand hurt; I was crying over being in another emergency room. I consoled myself by recalling that I was fully conscious and that I would not have to stay there.

In the circumstances, burning my hand was no idle accident. It indicated to me that I really did not want to play this role with my father. I did not want to assume the duties of my mother, did not want to serve him. Understanding this made me sad, for it meant that I had not yet fully accepted the past. As with the pneumonia, healing had occurred on some levels but not on others.

I was more than triumphant when I got through September. Only a year before, I had taken a massive overdose of pills and lain in a coma for three days. If the "death experience" of prolonged and deep unconsciousness can transform a soul, those three days should have done it. Also, my therapist was at the hospital, helping, from the time I arrived, making it a classic instance of attempted suicide from which I was rescued by my therapist. There have been cases where such circumstances resulted in a dramatic recovery, but no real change occurred in me.

Why not? I just wasn't ready yet. For one thing, I was drunk when I took the pills and do not recall swallowing them. I remember making the plan. Dave and I were taking the same medication, a combination of a tranquilizer and an antidepressant, and both prescriptions, as it happened, were refilled on the same day. Thus, there were almost 150 pills on hand. I intended taking them all, and I did take them all. However, I do not remember taking them, nor do I remember any conscious intention to die. Perhaps that is the reason my survival did not seem to be a major event. At that time, my therapist gave the clearest evidence possible of his commitment to me, but that commitment went unnoticed. If I was unable to make a commitment, I was also unable to receive one.

I faced the new September with some trepidation. It was a month of change. Would it change me? Would my upward spiral falter under the stresses of the season and the plunge toward Christmas? I wrote about beginnings and how they interlock with endings, and picked my way through the days as if I were walking on a tiny, narrow path set in a treacherous landscape.

The day my son went back to school, I felt very lonely. His school world was his own, and I was shut out of it. A friend told me recently that he would like to do his own thing if he could just figure out what it was, and I was in danger of feeling the same way. The days were waiting to be filled, and I hesitated before their emptiness. Then I saw that every detail of daily life, no matter how trivial, is open to extensive exploration and will yield its own meaning if you poke into it long enough. I began work on a long-term writing project.

When I passed the anniversary of that near-fatal suicide attempt, surviving a repetition of the circumstances which had triggered it, I knew I was safe, and I could survey the remainder of the year not only calmly but with enthusiasm. I gained confidence in my ability to survive, and survival itself became something special, even glorious. For a brief time, the Christmas season appeared ominous and I thought: In all this madness, there isn't any place for me, there isn't any little corner to which I can retreat and restore myself. But I was able to sort it out, put it in perspective; I found the little space I needed inside myself. Christmas became beautiful, because, no matter how busy I was, no matter how much I felt I was a tool of the season, I knew that in my heart I was at peace.

On New Year's Day, I called my sister to say, "I made it." There are many beautiful words in the English langauge, but those three, at that moment, were made of solid gold and were as large as the universe.

I made it, and I made it without alcohol. The day I came home from the hospital, Dave offered me a drink, part of our ritual of celebration, without which no event in our lives, whether momentous or trivial, could be confirmed. I took two swallows and knew it was not for me. My highly unstable mind could not tolerate alcohol; the fuzziness it induced almost immediately scared hell out of me. I had enough involuntary blurring without deliberately courting it. I put the glass down and thought, "Maybe some day I'll be able to drink normally, but not now."

I guess that's the dream of every alcoholic: Some day I'll be able to drink normally. Every day we try and every day normality eludes us. The day I can drink normally has not come, and it never will. I like the taste of alcohol, and I like the idea of drinking, but I just cannot drink. When I order a glass of wine with dinner, I drink about a third of it, and that is all I want. I don't like the effect of even that small amount. I used to think people who didn't drink were pretty dull sorts who didn't know what they were missing and were unwilling to find out. I know what I'm missing, and it is a country which no longer appeals to me. I thought I needed alcohol to relax before a party or to have a good time at one; I needed alcohol to boost my energy or get my day going; I needed alcohol to be more friendly or more clever or more interesting. I don't feel those needs any longer, and for me, the side effects of alcohol are losses.

I no longer enjoy drinking, and I guess the real question is: Why? I'm not sure I have the answer to that. When I was pregnant, I quit smoking because nicotine decreases the amount of oxygen in the bloodstream, thereby raising the specter of brain damage to the unborn child. I had smoked three packs a day, but I cut down to six cigarettes or less, thinking all the time that, as soon as the baby was born, I would take up smoking again.

The baby was born, but I did not resume my previous smoking pattern, because I couldn't. My craving was extreme, but when I lit a cigarette, I could take only two or three puffs and then I would have to put it out, because it tasted so terrible. More than terrible. Repulsive. For at least two years, I tried to smoke again and could not.

The real barrier, however, may have been something else. In the hospital, I had discovered that my keenest desire for a cigarette came when the baby was brought in to nurse at my breast. This association between breast-sucking and cigarette-smoking upset me. It seemed to me I wanted to smoke because I wanted to be a baby again. Cigarettes were substitutes for nipples or thumbs. At the same time, my attitude toward breast-feeding was ambivalent. I wanted to nurse my baby but could never provide enough milk. By the time he was a month old, I had to put him on bottles. I suspect I was a reluctant nurser because I did not want to be like my own mother, who had nursed me until I was almost a year old. In any case, I did not want to have anything to do with breast-sucking, real or surrogate, and I could no longer enjoy smoking, no matter how much my body demanded it.

The decision about alcohol was not so obvious. It had been clear for some time that alcohol was bad for me, that it encouraged my suicidal impulses and increased rather than alleviated my despair. Alcohol had been a factor in all but the first and the last of my suicide attempts. On one occasion—when I used carbon monoxide—I purposely got drunk in order to carry out my suicide plan.

But alcohol served other aims. I drank to get drunk, to hide, to escape. Alcohol blurred my pain and gave me a little lift, however temporarily. Although I did not go on binges, I was an alcoholic. Openly, I drank a great deal every day, but I also sneaked drinks whenever I could. The Madeira and the sherry we bought for cooking usually bypassed the cooking process on the way into my stomach. My ideal day began with a glass of champagne, and I suppose if it had ended there, it would have been all right, but it didn't. When the champagne was gone, I turned to what I called the "clean, clear taste of Scotch." If there was no Scotch, I turned to bourbon. Or rum. Or whatever. It didn't matter. At some point, I gave up hard liquor and drank only wine, but I drank enough of it to get the same result.

Like suicide, alcohol is a way of coping. Not a very good one, but something. My father could probably not survive without it. Blood chemistry is involved in the composition of an alcoholic, to be sure, but the psychological factors must also be present. I wanted, needed alcohol at that time, and no amount of intellectual persuasion could make any difference. Now, neither my body nor my psyche require this support, and, once again, reason has nothing to do with it. We think we are reasonable creatures, but reason must be allied with other forces within us before the whole person will turn.

I had to do my turning without the help of medication. Although the proposal that I go without drugs had originally been mine, I did not realize this embargo would have to be total. On my first night home from the hospital, I took a sleeping pill. I had not slept much while hospitalized, and I thought perhaps one good night's sleep was all I needed to put everything right and hold the focus in reality. How I missed those sleeping pills in the round-up of drugs for my suicide attempt, I don't know, but there were three of them in a bottle, and I took one. I slept all right, but when the alarm went off the next morning, I didn't know where I was or who I was or even what I was. I was so confused that I could not distinguish between the floor and the ceiling. Dave finally shut off the alarm and said, "Aren't you going to get up?" "In a minute," I said, and slowly, agonizingly summoned myself unto myself and got out of bed. No more sleeping pills.

In succeeding weeks, I sometimes slept no more than two hours a night. My therapist and I explored the subject of insomnia at some length, and there are lots of theories and lots of solutions, but every insomniac has to deal with the problem in his or her own way. For me, it has been helpful to accept sleeplessness as another—sometimes interesting—fact of life. If I cannot sleep, the worst thing to do is fight it, worrying about how dreadful I'm going to feel the next day. Proust describes this entire sequence very beautifully, and I often put myself to sleep by re-reading his description, accompanied by a glass of milk and something to eat. If you can't sleep, you can do something else. Putting down the anxiety caused by not sleeping is the main thing, and I have a little sentence I repeat to myself that accomplishes this for me: "At the center of every moment is a seed that is tranquil." Find the tranquil center of every moment. Then, even if you can't sleep, everything will be all right.

A few days after my bout with the sleeping pill, I got a severe headache and took an aspirin. One aspirin. In half an hour, I was in never-land, and the living room in which I was sitting turned to mush. All I could do was sit quietly and wait for the effects to wear off. I was terribly frightened that a single aspirin could have so profound a consequence. Obviously, I was still extraordinarily susceptible to drugs. Equally obviously, I would have to find some other way of dealing with headaches.

There is something about pain in my head that is far more threatening than pain in any other part of my body. My head is where I live. When pain invades it—the heavy, throbbing, burning pain of a severe headache—my entire presence seems to be in danger. In the past, I had taken heavy drugs for headaches: Codeine, Fiorinal, Demerol, Darvon. Usually they did not affect the headache, but, even when they did, they spaced me out. This was particularly true of Codeine. Thus, as my headache subsided, so did my contact with reality.

In my new circumstances, loss of reality was more to be feared than the pain of a headache. Even after my vulnerability to drugs wore off, my therapist and I decided we would explore other ways of dealing with my headaches. Consequently, I have been forced to try to understand them, to examine the circumstances in which they occur, and to identify exactly what is going on physiologically. If you have ever tried to localize pain, you will know how difficult this can be. "Where does it hurt?" says the doctor. "Well, down around there, sort of." Or, "All over." Or, "Right in the gut." In general terms, that may be where it hurts. Specifically, the source of the pain may actually be somewhere else, and it sometimes takes some pretty fancy detective work to figure out where that is.

In the case of my headaches, I have made many discoveries with the aid of biofeedback training. Muscle tension is sometimes involved, for example. I feel the pain in my head, but the muscles which trigger that pain are in my neck and shoulders. Learning to relax those muscles has virtually eliminated that type of headache. There is also a vascular component; the blood vessels in the scalp swell and become engorged with blood. It has been found that people who suffer from vascular headaches have a marked difference in temperature between the skin of the forehead and the skin of the hands. (Maybe the saying should be: Cold hands, warm head.) So, I have been learning to increase the temperature of my hands through biofeedback. At the same time, I am learning not to be afraid of headaches, much as I learned not to be afraid of sleeplessness. As a result, they no longer wipe me out as they once did.

Other problems which drugs might have alleviated still plagued me. My anxiety level was so high that it rattled my teeth. Certainly, no one was going to give me a tranquillizer, so I did not ask for one. Gritting those rattling teeth as best I could, I took my one step at a time in the here and now. When I was not too frightened, I tried to track my anxiety down to its source. Some of those first discoveries were truly illuminating.

There was my discomfort about having people depend on me. All my life, whenever anyone became dependent on me, I cut out. That was the real reason I left my first husband—his dependence stifled me. I think I would have left Dave had it not been for our son, but the presence of a dependent child created a terrible conflict for me. I could leave Dave, but not the boy. On the other hand, I could not leave Dave and keep the boy, because I would simply have been taking the conflict with me. At one point, I wrote: "I am caught between an old man who is my husband and a young man who is my son, and I float between them in perfumed isolation."

At the time, I did not realize it was the dependence of both husband and son that was oppressing me. All I knew was that I couldn't stay and I couldn't go. I was caged like some animal and did not know how to open the gate. So I took the only way that was visible to me, over and over and over, trying to force a change in a situation I had helped create but could not tolerate. It is a curious pattern, in which I say: You must rely on me, but if you do, I shall resent it.

I had a kind of eclectic amnesia. In the first part of this book, I wrote that electrotherapy had not affected my memory much, but I am not sure that is true. I began bumping into situations where other people remembered events I did not remember, although I had participated in them. My sister reminded me of a trip we made together. I remembered nothing about it, although it lasted for two days. Not the faintest glimmer of a picture came to my mind when she discussed that trip.

On another occasion, my son and I met a friend for lunch in a restaurant I thought I had never seen before. As we walked in, he said, "Oh, I've eaten here before." "When?" I asked in surprise. "Last summer," he replied, "with you and two of your friends. We went to an art gallery afterwards." The restaurant and the circumstances were totally unfamiliar to me.

This memory loss is not the same as ordinary forgetting. When you forget something and someone reminds you of it, you then recall it. Your memory of it may not be the same as the other person's, but at least you can identify it. My forgetting was of a different order. My feeling about the trip with my sister, the visit to the restaurant, and various other events, was not that I had forgotten them, but that they had never occurred. When I go to consult the file, it just isn't there, and I feel a curious sense of vacancy. If it isn't there, where is it?

Amnesia associated with electrotherapy usually covers the period immediately preceding and during the treatments, but I have memory gaps concerning events which occurred months afterward. This leads me to speculate that the drug overdoses I took also affected my memory mechanism. After my experience in the county hospital, I was worried about permanent brain damage. Could this flickering instability of reality be a phenomenon I would have to deal with for the rest of my life? But those disorders of perception subsided, and it is possible that events currently missing from my memory will one day be found, also. Perhaps I have only lost the ability to recall them, the clue as to where they are filed, and that may eventually be restored.

We talk a lot about having compassion for others—compassion for the world's poor, the starving, the ugly. And that is relatively easy. Our hearts go out to the orphan, the refugee, the bewildered survivor of some horrible disaster. But turning that compassion toward ourselves is another matter. We have trouble accepting our own poverty, starvation, and ugliness. Somehow, it is much easier to forgive the person who attempts suicide and succeeds than the one who attempts it and fails.

My therapist once asked me what I wanted from him, and when I had thought about it for some time, I said I wanted his forgiveness. Actually, his forgiveness would not have resolved anything; what I really needed was my own forgiveness. That image of myself standing over the bathroom sink lifting and lowering the razor blade haunted me like a scene from an insane movie. I wanted to erase it, wipe it out, forget it, but I had to remember it, pull it into my person, forgive it. We suffer our harshest judgments from ourselves, and sometimes cannot live with them.

My own self-judgment was black and unforgiving, a verdict without appeal, but I have at last turned away from it. How did that come about? Nothing in my external circumstances had changed. My husband still had a chronic illness for which there was apparently no remedy, and he was deteriorating physically. Although my son was growing up and away, he still needed me. Husband and son had not changed, our life situation had not changed, and, for that matter, I had not changed in any way that most people would recognize. I was still the same person, with the same faults and virtues, the same face, the same history. However, I was coming to terms with that person. I was learning to know her, to accept her, and to put her all together into some kind of integrated whole. All the fragments I had felt were so loosely assembled without meaning or purpose were beginning to fit together. I could be who I was because of what I had been, and what I had been was part of who I was. The process was exciting and beautiful.

I had always had trouble with my name. What's your name? was not an easy question to answer. The name I was born into was strange and foreign; the other kids couldn't understand it, and they laughed at it. My grandparents came to this country with Lithuanian names, unspellable and unpronounceable. When my paternal grandfather presented himself to the immigration officials, his name baffled them, and rather than try to record it correctly, they transliterated it into something that would have been as strange and foreign in Lithuania as it was in the United States. Therefore, my name did not even have the dignity of being authentic. It was a bastard name, and I hated it.

My first husband's name was not much of an improvement. It was a nice German-Jewish name, but it had too many syllables and was unmusical in English. Because it was so obviously Jewish, I was asked to use another name when I worked for the Government of Pakistan.

Now I had three names: my maiden name, my married name, and the name I used at work. After the divorce, I had a choice of names, but I did not want any of those, so I took the name, Mary Savage, which I have used for all my writing. My second marriage added another name to the string, so that when someone asks me what my name is, I could very well say: "Which one?"

But names are important; they identify us to the world, and I think one of the reasons women have identity problems is that they are required to take their husbands' names. Be that as it may, my lack of a permanent name troubled me. Recently, I forgot to do some things I had promised to do, which upset me because, although I don't always do what I have said I would, it isn't because I forget about it. Then I dreamt I had forgotten something really important, and when I asked myself what it could be, the answer was: my name.

The series of names I used reflected my deep sense of personal fragmentation. With one name, I was one person; with another name, I was another person, but no solid connections linked these various persons. Thus, I had to look at all of my names and at the people they belonged to and incorporate them into what I am now. I am that Lithuanian child, that Jewish wife, that public relations person, that copywriter, that mother. I am also that sick woman who had no name.

This process of integration, of assimilation, was inherent in my psychotherapy. I had been in therapy for two years prior to my rough landing in the county hospital. Watching my downward spiral, my husband wondered what all this therapy was doing besides enriching my therapist. But "all this therapy," including my LSD experience, was like planting seeds in a garden. You don't see them growing for a long time, and then suddenly something sprouts. The discussions, the analyses, the insights achieved at one level or another in my mind found their places in the structure of my person.

Prior to my last suicide attempt, there had always been some barrier to this process, preventing the lessons from being thoroughly assimilated. Something shattered that barrier, or perhaps it dissolved slowly and only seemed to be suddenly gone. Whatever happened, it resulted in a deeper willingness to learn. But why didn't it go the other way? When I found myself in the county hospital—another failure to my credit, alone and suffering from pneumonia in an unsympathetic environment—why didn't I interpret this as further proof of my essential rottenness, by lack of worth, my spiritual depravity?

I don't really know, but I keep coming back to the fact that this time I had committed myself to death as fully as I had ever committed myself to anything, and it had not worked. Now I had to commit myself to life, first as an act of desperation but later as an act of love. Like a rat that finally stops banging its head against a gate that never opens, I would stop committing a suicide that never let me out. I would accept the fact that whatever I was doing, I was not committing suicide. I would learn to live not as an automaton or a collection of fragments but as a whole person, more alive in every particle than I had ever been.

When we talk about this, Dave says, "But you did it yourself." And I agree. I did it myself. Without my decision to live, I might very well be dead by now. But doing it myself is not the same as doing it *by* myself. I could not have done it alone. I needed a guide, a teacher, a therapist.

Since I was sixteen—or maybe it began when I was nine—I had been tangling with recurring cycles of depression and despair. At the hospital, I came to a crisis. Would that crisis and its outcome have been possible without everything that had preceded it? I have thought about this a lot, and my answer is, "No." I had to go all the way down the road before I could come back up. I had to explore the full measure of despair, including the acts of suicide, before I could emerge from it. I had to go the whole dark, destructive route, living it all the way to the end and ultimately experiencing a kind of death, before I could find the light again and fully realize myself. If that was what was required to make me well, I could not have made it all the way through without psychotherapy.

The journey nearly killed me, but now I am alive, wonderfully, gratefully, reverentially alive. And I ask myself whether I did not know all the time—somewhere inside my mind, somewhere tucked into one of those tiny jewel boxes of information which were locked for so long—that I would survive. Some months after my discharge from the county hospital, when it was clear that my recovery was certain, my therapist commented that when I came back to him for treatment the second time, the fat was in the fire. I did not know it then, but I was making a commitment—an awesome, terrible commitment that involved the pursuit of my own death.

Timing was essential—and mysterious. Why did the seed sprout today and not yesterday? Consider the matter of my feelings toward my mother, especially my anger which was so thoroughly covered up that I did not know it was there. My therapist urged me to discover this anger, to express it within the safe boundaries of his office. But I would not. Prior to the last suicide attempt, we were probing the question of my anger toward him, which I denied.

"No," I said vehemently, "I'm not angry." I did not feel anger, even though I could recognize intellectually that I was exhibiting it. The admission of anger might lead to the admission of hatred. I did not hate the therapist, and I did not hate my mother. My mother had done nothing to elicit anything as strong as hatred. She may not have been a very good mother, but she tried. She may have made mistakes, but she was doing her best. After all, I was now a mother and could understand her problems. No, I wasn't angry. No, I didn't hate my mother. It was not possible. It was not justified. Let's all please be rational about our mothers.

But I could hate myself, so I chopped up my wrist with a razor blade and then decided to die. Yes, Mother, I really do hate you. I hate you so much that I don't want to live any more.

One day, while working on this book, I was considering the above circumstances. What did it all mean, really? I knew about the anger, but only as an observer. Sometimes when you look up at the sky, you see the clouds rushing along, shifting, changing, tossing, and you conclude that, up there, the wind is blowing.

But it isn't blowing where you are standing and you do not feel it. That was the way it was with my anger.

As I was thinking about this, all of a sudden the wind moved down and hit me right in the chest. Anger. Anger billowed up in me like a thundercloud. Mother, Mother, what did you do to me? You took my feelings away from me. You stole them and hid them so completely that I couldn't find them again. You laughed at me for having feelings, so I began concealing them from myself—concealing them, confusing them, mistrusting them. They got all wound up into a weird kind of ball which I could only carry around with me in a lump, to be produced on occasion, usually inappropriately. Because they were so compressed, they became intense and frightening.

I sat down and wrote a poem about it, addressed to my mother. It contained a great deal of resentment, bitterness and hatred. But I did not understand what was in the poem when I wrote it. Perhaps I did not dare to understand it. I put the poem in my handbag, and I tried to put the feelings in the handbag along with it.

Several days later, I took the poem to my therapist. As he read it, I was assailed by grief. Grief for my mother because she had aroused these feelings in me. Grief because I knew she had not meant to do what she had done to me, and I was sorry I had found out about it. I grieved over her tragedy, and I grieved for my own.

The therapist looked up. "Why do you find this so frightening?" he asked. Frightening? I wasn't frightened, I was sad. "It might get out of control," I whispered, remembering. He shook his head. "Now that you know it's there, you can draw on it; it's energy you can use." My anger and hatred had been dangerous only as long as they were under pressure. Now they were exposed and available.

But I still felt sad. Poor, tired, sick woman. She had not been directly involved in my life for thirty years; why should I still hate her so much? "Out of hatred comes sadness," my son had said, and I felt the truth of that observation. But he had also said, "Out of hatred comes knowledge."

"You loved her too," my therapist reminded me, "and the opposite of love is not hate, but indifference." All my life I had been striving for indifference, trying to suppress any emotion only to have it pop out again where least expected. I could not bear to love my mother, because I could not bear to find out that I also hated her. Mother, Mother, Mother, you are still sitting on my shoulder.

The therapist told me I would probably feel a great many emotions about my mother because of this discovery and might have strange fantasies about her, like the little boy who wrote that he wanted to drive nails into his mother's eyes and throw her in the garbage can. It was a Pandora's box, and I had lifted the cover.

That night, my old fear of the dark temporarily returned. Why should I be afraid? I thought. What was going on? It was several days before I learned the reason for my fear. In the meantime, I was subject to turbulent emotions, ranging from joy to grief, love to sickness, fear to freedom. Regret and apology: I didn't want it to be this way, Mom. I'm sorry, I'm sorry. I wept because when I tried to remember her as she was, I could not recall anything good about her, no tenderness, no understanding, no illumined photograph like the ones you see in magazines. There were only scenes of criticism, ridicule, and hurt. But you loved me, Mom. I know you did. Why can't I remember that?

At the same time, a part of me was waking up that had been asleep for a long, long time. As I felt each of these emotions, it became accessible to me in a new way. I could feel love and joy and sadness and know that each feeling was valid, was my own, was genuine. Newly awake, these emotions no longer derived from my mother.

Fear threatened me from time to time. I knew now that my anger would not become rage, but I was not sure whether or not my fear might become panic. Out of control, fear is just as destructive as anger. Finally, I understood the reason for my fear: it was a fear of loss. Mother had been sitting on my shoulder all my life, judging me. By expressing my true feelings for her, by making them my own, I was taking away her power and might lose her. If I did not need her any more, she would be destroyed; her destruction would be my fault, and I would be left alone with my guilt. I had depended upon her to inform my being, but she had also depended upon me to affirm hers. In breaking that interdependence, we might both be lost.

Nevertheless, I had to let go of her; there was nothing else to do. In one of my dreams, my mother and I were at an airport where I was trying to catch a plane. I was hampered by the fact that she had both legs in casts, and I had to half-carry, half-drag her up and down flights of stairs and along corridors to the loading area. As long as she encumbered me, I would never catch that plane.

In the end, I did not lose anything, I rearranged it. My mother was still a part of me, but she was no longer in control of me. I could acknowledge her, but I need not obey her. It was as if a layer of ice around my heart had melted, making me at the same time more vulnerable and more secure. So long, Mom, I don't need you—as a point of reference—any more. From then on, my experience of myself was a deeper, truer one, but the only place I had dared to expose its beginnings was in the therapist's office.

The process of psychotherapy is not usually so obvious. The events described above happened fairly late in the proceedings, and represent a culmination of many hours of hard work. I could not achieve this insight earlier because I wasn't ready for it, and as far as I know there are no shortcuts.

The poet Rilke once said he was afraid of psychotherapy because, although it might dispose of his devils, it might also annihilate his angels. For a long time, I halfway believed he was right, but I don't think so any more. Psychotherapy reveals one's devils, to be sure, but it does not necessarily require jettisoning them. If you shake hands with the devil, you not only rob him of his ability to do harm, you may also enlist his strength in the service of other goals.

As for angels, it is exciting to discover that they do, indeed, exist, but it is not true that to be effective an angel must remain anonymous. If one regards an angel as creative inspiration, as Rilke must have, shining a little light on it will not destroy it.

Thus, when I write a poem or paint a picture, I am calling upon both my angels and my devils to help me express something—whether a humorous observation or a fresh insight or a desire to tidy up leftovers. In the past, I threw much of my writing away, but I realize now that in so doing, I was discarding that part of myself from which it sprang, saying it was no good and did not merit preservation. Today, my writing is the primary way in which I speak my life—just as, for some women, it is the house or the garden. In it, I pull together the various roles I play throughout the day and bring them into perspective.

For a long time, I thought I really wasn't anything. If you unwrapped me like an onion, as that first psychiatrist wanted to do, you would not find anything at all, except perhaps a transient smell—and not a particularly pleasant one. Now I know I have a center. I am really here, and I can say so. My voice may not be loud or strong, but it has its own significance. I am my own meaning.

Thus, I have recovered from what seems, in retrospect, to have been a lifelong illness. Not only have I come back from the clinical depression I was suffering when I entered the county hospital, but I have also made a deeper, more meaningful turning. I have turned away from the darkness that was the backdrop for my depression, the darkness that made my entire life seem purposeless and incoherent. Not that the darkness no longer exists; it is still there, but it is not the canvas on which my life is painted.

This is the change, this deep and private turning, that has made it possible for me to go on living. Not surviving, but living.

It represents a willingness to deal with life as it comes, and is a basic change in my point of view, enabling me to learn and grow, to assemble and be who I am.

I don't know exactly how this change came about. There were many factors: psychotherapy, electrotherapy, pneumonia, biochemistry, prolonged unconscious (which may have entailed a death exerience), time. Combine all of these elements in the individual who was lying on that bed in the county hospital, and something happened, something which had not happened before even when those same elements, as isolated events, were already a part of my experience.

My theory is that timing was vital. Taken in context, one event leads to another, making the outcome seem inevitable. Given my previous history and my present circumstances, what other result could there have been? Was my survival inevitable? If I had died, my death would have seemed just as inevitable. If I had lived but continued to attempt suicide, that would have seemed inevitable, too. There might indeed be a "time to die," and mine has not yet arrived; if it had, my suicide would have been a confirmation of it.

Whatever one's theory, I suffered a crisis of the soul while I was in the county hospital. At some instant, probably while I was still unconscious, everything came together with a force that shattered something within me. My old way of looking at life was destroyed just as surely as if I had actually died and returned.

Thus it was that I was able to make a commitment to living which I had been unable to make before. And thus it was, with this commitment still in embryonic form, that I came to read *The Varieties of Religious Experience* during my last days in the hospital. The book had been lent to me previously by a dear friend who, on reading the first part of this manuscript, found in it certain similarities to the intense experiences described by James, especially the association between madness and religious ecstasy. I did not read it when he first gave it to me, probably because I was not ready.

From the age of six when my mother gave me my first book of nursery rhymes, books have been important to me and have influenced various turning points in my life. For example, reading *The Second Sex* by Simone de Beauvoir contributed to my decision to divorce my first husband. James' book had an equal impact. Drawing his material from first-hand reports, he wrote convincingly of how the force we sometimes call God had presented itself to various people at various times, transforming and strengthening them. No matter how strange the experience seemed, they could not deny its reality. Although such enlightenments can sometimes be subverted and misused, their original direction is always positive: nobility of spirit, inner peace, unshakable confidence.

Was it possible, I wondered, that something like that had happened to me? There, in that midnight of my life, had I encountered a force which is the source of being? Was that the reason I was now able to see, where I had previously been blind?

The day after coming home from the hospital, I got up early to send my son off to school. After he was gone, I knelt on the floor, folded my hands and said, "Thank you. I am come home unto myself." My eyes were closed, tears streamed down my cheeks, I was shaking. Then I felt something—or someone—touch my face, very gently, and with great warmth, affirmation and welcome.

When I described the incident to my therapist, I said, "Far out." "To whom?" he replied.

As a child, I was completely alienated from religion. Going to church or Sunday school was the dullest thing anyone could possibly do. I pictured God as an old man with a beard, wearing a biblical robe and sitting at a huge desk, making notes in a ledger on everyone's behavior, with appropriate comments as to its "morality." I thought heaven must be a pretty terrible place because no one ever slept there, and I could visualize myself in heaven trying to stay awake and finally falling asleep and falling out.

When I was eighteen, I had a brief fling with the Roman Catholic Church. All of my grandparents came from a Roman Catholic country, and the women were devout churchgoers. (The men were devout drunks.) Baptized "in the church" and often left in the care of one of my grandmothers, I had been thoroughly exposed to Catholicism while quite small. My parents, however, acted religious only at Easter and Christmas. My father was uncomfortable in church (as well as in a movie theatre) because he suffered the fear of being in an enclosed space with a crowd of people. Whatever religion he practiced had to be out in the open and by himself. Mother believed that without some kind of religion, one would be eternally damned. Both rebelled against Catholicism; my father, at one point, professed to be a Christian Scientist, and Mother wound up a Lutheran.

After my first sojourn in a mental hospital, I attended services in a tiny chapel attached to a Roman Catholic college near our home. I went to six-o'clock mass on Sunday mornings, walking across dawn-damp meadows and feeling good about the Sundays of my life. The service was entirely in Latin and there was no sermon. I loved the beauty and serenity of the ritual, unlittered by lectures on sin and damnation and hellfire. These services were what religion should be: a matter of the heart. I had a sense of quiet communion with something unidentified.

This seedling romance withered when I went to New York and began reading philosophy and asking questions. I delved into Episcopal beliefs, but it was an intellectual inquiry which never bore fruit. One can very easily get bogged down in definitions and never get beyond them.

Then there was my conversion to Judaism, which I justified as a matter of necessity, but which was probably also an indication that I wanted some kind of spiritual life. I loved the rabbi who instructed me in Judaic principles, and I wanted to practice Jewish ritual at home. My husband said I wanted to be more Jewish than the Jews.

For a number of years I worked for the Consulate General of Pakistan in New York, where I became acquainted with the teachings of Islam. I particularly admired the Pakistani Foreign Minister, who came to New York for sessions of the U.N. General Assembly. He was a devout Muslim, as well as a brilliant debater, and I worked with him occasionally. He talked to me about his religion and gave me books to read. But Muslims and Jews are not happy partners, and I found it hard to equate the principles of Islam with its expression in national policy.

At some point, I became too sophisticated to talk about God. The word itself got in the way. I could talk about a "life force" or a "unifying spirit" or a "supreme consciousness," but call any of these things God, and Chunk! down came the gate. "I do not believe in a personal God," I said, remembering that old man frowning over his judgments. "Nor do I believe in personal survival after death. When I die, that which I call 'I' vanishes completely." In trying to commit suicide, I was trying to snuff out the "I" whose presence in this world was far too painful.

But God was very much involved in my experience with LSD. There was a presence in the room, over, above and around everyone and everything that was visible. We were all aware of it, but I felt it was something generated by my unconscious. Moreover, I was annoyed because God was always represented as a man; when I looked at a painting of the crucifixion, I saw Christ as a woman with a mustache, "a harlot," I said. One day, some weeks afterward, I was sitting on the floor in our living room listening to Verdi's "Requiem." The music filled me with light, and I felt radiant and buoyant, uplifted and bathed in some sort of incandescence. It seemed, then, that the hand of God reached down to bless me, but I said, "No. Give that to my mother." My mother was going into the hospital the next day for gall bladder surgery.

Despite this perception of a spiritual presence, I continued to regard God as an intellectual matter. It was interesting to speculate about this presence, but it had no significance in my interior health. I had seen too much hypocrisy as a child. People behaved virtuously for an hour on Sunday; the rest of the time, they were their old muddy, grubby selves, and this included those who were allegedly devoted to a spiritual life. When one tested to find out if the voice spoke truly, one found that the words came from no deeper source than the back of the throat; the priest or minister appeared to be far more interested in what you put into the collection plate than in what you put into your own soul.

Deep down, however, I think I could not acknowledge God's presence because I felt I was not worthy of that presence. I had always felt I would not survive any kind of thorough self-scrutiny. Psychotherapy frightened me because I was convinced it would reveal an innate psychosis, a madness beyond redemption. My experience with LSD didn't help, because of the difficulty I had in reassembling myself afterward. Feeling that I had narrowly escaped destruction by LSD, I feared that any further attempt to explore my inner being might plunge me into the abyss. Therefore, to say, "God, here I am," was to invite condemnation. If God saw me, he would either laugh or look the other way, for my central core was rottenness, beyond which there was nothing.

My therapist had long urged me to explore religion, but no formal religion could survive my critical appraisal. Meditation was suggested, but again I was afraid that any inner search would produce only goblins, whose presence I would not be able to bear.

And so I talked and read and thought but did not move.

When I came home from the county hospital, I had to move. Whatever the reason for my recovery, it was imperative that it be reinforced. It might be merely a matter of biochemistry, but I had to find some means of coping with the fear of a recurrence of chemical imbalance even if lithium were to be used. I had discovered that there was a spark in me, something that would not let me die, and I wanted to foster it, help it grow. It had been there all the time, but I had chosen to ignore it or had been only peripherally aware of it. The time had come to make it central.

I looked around for a way to do this. Psychotherapy was helping me to recognize and resolve my conflicts; painting was helping me to relax and explore new perceptions; writing was helping me to stabilize my identity. But the central spark of life required nourishment of a different sort. Referring to James, it seemed that a religious framework was needed, if I could find one that was comfortable and did not offend my intellectual criteria too violently.

I experimented with several religions, going to churches and listening. In the end, I found I brought too much negative feeling with me to truly listen to a Western religion. So I chose an Eastern one which stresses meditation. There, with a teacher, I learned to listen to another part of myself, and, through that listening, make contact with the source of my own life-spark. This source has been given many names, but the shortest and most satisfactory is Om, or God.

I don't care how you define God. I think all definitions are correct, and, at the same time, none is, for in the process of formulating a definition, you confine something that is essentially unconfinable. Also, any definition becomes a basis for argument. The best description of God I have come across is the one that says God is a circle whose circumference is nowhere but whose center is everywhere.

Very early in my practice of meditation, I experienced the cliché that God is love. It could also be called energy. It flowed through me like a soft fire, a slow current that ignited everything it touched, imbuing it with tremendous power which was at the same time the epitome of peace. My first reaction was: I am loved. I, even I, this formerly worthless, lost, lost thing. And I knew that no life is meaningless, not even mine.

When I was going through the turbulence about my mother, I found this limitless expanse of love every time I sat down to meditate, and it strengthened my willingness to deal with my thoughts about her and expose my feelings toward her. It was an unqualified love—permanent and indestructible. I knew I could call upon it at any time, in any place. It was not Out There somewhere, but inside, always available.

This, then, is my insurance against dark days and bleak landscapes. My life is no easier or more difficult than any other person's, and the road I walk is occasionally full of potholes and subject to flash floods. I do not get up singing every morning, and there are times when my inner peace is pretty well fogged in. There are days when I feel as tightly stretched as an inflated balloon, and others when the balloon has been punctured.

But, for the first time in my life, there is the knowledge that I have a center. My inner being, somehow or other, will suffice, and that spark will continue to glow within me as long as my life needs it. In my heart, I am glad I am alive, even on those days when I don't understand what life is all about. Today, I will learn something. It's all right if I forget to feed the cats.

Thus am I truly come home.

*When a high wind blows
that we see but cannot feel,
there are clouds whispering
across my soul, visible/
invisible/untouchable sifting
through my fingers like moonbeams*

*There are bird wings flapping
in my heart, in the turbulence
of dawn, turned-on dawn,
daylight rising in some
unbearable glory,
birdwings singing hawks/
falcons/finches
rising from the slow tears
turning in my bewildered heart.*

*Oh my soul,
you are awaking
from your long and silent sleep,
springing to catch the
high wind blowing and the
clouds are weeping their
heaviness
out of their deep deep
need for grief.*

*I feel the wild birds flapping
their wings whipped by the storm
as they shriek their
joy and cry their
pain and twist and curl
in the high wind's beckoning blast.*

*Oh my soul,
you are awake
on this new day of my
remembering,
your crystal flame
has been ignited
and the high birds flap
their golden wings
in the windsong
of scattering clouds
and the tear-moist soil
is ready for a new birth.*

AFTERWORD

SOMETIMES, during the last five years, I wondered if I had learned anything at all from my experience. I had to deal with grief, loss, depression and renewed suicidal feelings. It seemed that instead of moving forward I had merely completed another circle. But the fact is that it has now been five years since I have attempted suicide or been hospitalized for depression. I have survived, not perhaps as a sun-kissed daisy, but at least as a clump of tough old grass. I have demonstrated that my commitment to life is genuine under the stress of adverse circumstances, both inner and outer. Therefore, I was pleased to be asked to write an Afterword to a book which describes a trip into the depths and out again.

It is difficult to describe depression to someone who has never experienced it. It is not just a matter of feeling low or down or in a bad mood. It is a matter of darkness that wipes out all color, of anxiety that terrifies and immobilizes, of pain that seeps through every pore in the body. I would rather have any physical pain I have ever experienced ten times over than suffer a single day of the pain of depression. When I am depressed, I feel diseased, cancerous, invaded by some alien chemical, and I long to externalize it. I would prefer to have a broken leg or a heart attack or some other physical problem that is recognizable, visible, discussable; I would prefer to have something with an acknowledged beginning, prognosis, and ending.

This was the state that descended on me once again some six months after this book was published. It seemed to me depression had been lying in wait like a burglar behind a door. One day I was busy, happy, working, secure, and the next day the room had no floor. It was as sudden and surprising as that. I felt especially victimized because I had not been drinking, and had in fact been struggling to make amends to my husband and son for the heartache I had caused them during the severe, suicidal phase of my earlier illness. I did not see that I had once again been aiming too high, striving for perfection when a day-to-day willingness to live was all that was needed. I made the mistake of thinking that life could be shaped into a nice round ball, stuck with cloves and tied with a ribbon, like a pomander. I thought that because I had suffered and survived, I would now have peace and joy as my lifetime companions, that the end of my illness was permanent, that the spiritual awakening I had felt would protect me from all subsequent sorrow.

I thought I was special. When I was sick, exceptions were to be made for me because I was so sick. When I was well—so exuberant as to be almost manic—I thought I deserved special rewards. Extra space was to be given to me because I had cried, and tried, so hard. I was wrong. Learning the lesson of that error cost me months of anguish and despair, months during which I started drinking again, made suicide plans again, neglected self and family again.

This repetition of all the old responses filled me with anger and dismay. I went back to my psychotherapist. "What's happening?" I asked. "I've done all the right things, but everything's going sour. I feel as though I've slipped and now am on the downward side of the spiral." He listened and after due consideration put me on antidepressant medication. The fact that I was on medication after having been totally free of it for a year and a half saddened me. When I told him I was suicidal, he said, "That's part of the disease, a symptom," and I felt better. Somehow regarding those feelings as mere symptoms made them easier to deal with. I did not have to act on a symptom, I could just sit back and watch it.

Nevertheless, there were days in which I had to fight actively the desire to commit suicide. I did this by various means: I called friends; I painted; I visited bright cheerful anonymous places like supermarkets and gift shops, and I reread this book. The book represented a promise I had made never to try suicide again, a sort of gauntlet flung down in the face of depression, a hostage that guaranteed my life. I might not be able to do anything about the depression, but I could adhere to the vow once made on paper that I would not take the ultimate way out.

Those are not startlingly dramatic techniques. I did not run or jog or eliminate sugar from my diet. I had done such things but have not found them useful as tools to fight depression. A change of focus was what was required, even so slight a change as a geographic movement.

There was also my son. I cannot overrate his importance in helping me to fight depression and suicidal thinking. Following my recovery from the last hospital experience, my therapist suggested we arrange for therapy for the boy. He and I were quarreling fiercely and frequently; I felt that my suicide attempts had been corrosive. When it became obvious that I was no longer suicidal, the time seemed right to help him understand himself and his relationship with me.

He began sessions with a therapist who specialized in children and was in therapy on a semi-weekly basis for about a year. Dave and I had short sessions with the therapist after each of our son's visits. My son was—and is—a brilliant but shy boy, one who finds it difficult to let other people get close to him. With the therapist's help we grew to understand some of our ambivalence toward each other. My youngster grew better able to let other people into his life.

Because of my experiences with my own mother, I often doubted my own mothering abilities. I was constantly fearful of repeating her mistakes and yet, because she was my role-model, I repeated them anyway. My son and I had what the psychologists call a "symbiotic relationship." We were too close, too involved with each other, too dependent. The therapist stressed the necessity of keeping our boundaries separate and distinct. It was as simple as saying, "This is where I end and you begin."

I found it terribly difficult. Even today I have difficulty separating my feelings from his. He is 13 now and becoming increasingly independent. In spite of my knowledge of the essential nature of such a development, I find it threatening. I love the boy deeply and yet every time he sets out in some new direction, I hold my breath and long to hold him back. I want to protect him from the pain of life, and yet I know that no growth is possible without pain. I spend a lot of energy trying not to interfere.

He helps me in this maturing process. I am grateful that he is much more self-protective than I was as a child. I know things that my mother never suspected about parent-child relationships, but in spite of that knowledge I find myself striving to be the perfect mother with the perfect child. It is a heavy burden for my son, as well as for me, but the sessions with the therapist helped him not only during that time but also during the events that were to follow.

For my drinking, I turned to Alcoholics Anonymous. I found I had sufficient faith to give up alcohol one day at a time. I was truly terrified not only by the fact that I was using alcohol but also by the way I was using it. I became a "secret" drinker, trying to hide my consumption from myself as well as others, being careful to keep my distance from other people toward the end of the day so that they would not smell the evidence on my breath. Finding a group whose experiences with alcohol were similar to mine and who had put their lives together coherently and kept them that way gave me hope and courage.

My husband's health continued to fail. He seemed to be wasting away in front of my eyes and he became increasingly unsteady on his feet. On a trip we made to Colorado in 1975 he fell and broke his arm; the following year he fell on the stairs and broke his collarbone. By Thanksgiving 1976 his balance was so precarious and his general feeling of malaise so marked that I insisted he see a doctor, which he finally agreed to do early in December. The doctor examined him and had X-rays made of his chest. A day later he called me with the news: "There's a mass in his left lung that could be cancer. Whatever it is, it isn't good."

At my and the doctor's insistence, Dave went into the hospital on December 19th for further tests. On December 22nd, we were informed that it was indeed lung cancer and on the 27th that it had metastasized into his bones and his brain. Surgery was out of the question; radiation and chemotherapy might extend his life somewhat. Dave vehemently refused such measures. He was given three to six months to live and was brought home from the hospital on December 30th.

By the time he came home from the hospital, he could not walk without assistance and then only a few steps. I had arranged for a hospital bed to be set up in the guest room and a handyman rigged up a bell arrangement so that Dave could signal whenever he wanted me. We settled down to our vigil.

Throughout, Dave was fully cognizant of his condition, and we were equally frank with our son. The three of us were drawn together in a bond of closeness such as we had not known before. We were honest about our feelings and did everything we could to support each other. The only outside assistance we had was from the Visiting Nurse Association who sent a registered nurse to check Dave's condition and to counsel me. They also sent a practical nurse to bathe him and wash his hair. My friends were beautiful. Nearly every day one of them came by to have lunch with me or to sit with Dave while I went shopping or on other errands.

In the beginning, I was able to sleep upstairs in our bed, relying on the bell arrangement if Dave should waken or need assistance during the night. As time went by, however, his right arm became useless and I slept on a sofa in the room with him. Our son elected to sleep on the floor in a sleeping bag. On many nights, a strong wind blew, rattling the window panes and brushing the tree branches against the side of the house. I would lie awake, listening to the wind and the sounds of my husband's breathing.

One night he asked me if there were anything I wanted to say to him before he died. I thought for a long time. How could I put it into words? I had loved him deeply and yet I had been a source of pain. I had wanted to be a good wife, a perfect wife, and yet I had shouted and cursed and failed to give him all the understanding he needed. "I'm sorry I wasn't a better wife," I said at last.

He smiled as if it were a matter of no importance. "I'm ready to die," he said. "I've done everything I wanted to do; I've had a long, full life."

He suffered little physical pain, but a great deal of mental anguish because of his inability to express himself. The thoughts were clear enough in his mind, but became jumbled in the speech center and it became very difficult to understand him. One morning when he awoke, he told me he had been trying to die all night. "Why can't I die?" he managed to say.

He grew confused. He spoke often of wanting to go home and would try to get out of bed, intent on some destination outside the room. Over and over again, he would mumble, "I want to go home, I want to go home," but when we tried to find out just what he meant, he was unable to tell us. He seemed to hate the bed he was in and would grimace when I put up the side rails at night. I hated doing this, but I was afraid he might fall out of bed in his restlessness. One morning he said to me, "I was in Hell last night. There were demons after me."

Dave's ex-wife and his daughter (and her husband and little girl) had to be summoned. They arrived on the night of Sunday, January 30th, and they stayed until Tuesday afternoon. It was a difficult time—"bittersweet," his ex-wife later called it. By this time, Dave's speech problems were so acute that I was the only one who could understand him, and that but a part of the time. Each member of the family, except the 5-year-old, spent some time privately with Dave, and once the son-in-law carried him out to the living room to sit in his favorite chair for half an hour. His ex-wife and I managed to fit in a visit to the attorney to discuss the terms of Dave's will.

This visit, for all its harried nature, seemed to settle something for Dave. It was as though he had now said good-bye to all the people he cared about and there were no more obstacles to his dying.

He died quietly and beautifully on Friday, February 4, 1977. His death marked the beginning of a very painful year for me. Despite the dissension and unhappiness that were so much a part of our relationship during the last years of his life, we had been deeply committed to each other. In one role or another, he had been intimately involved in my life for some 39 years. His departure left a vacancy which nothing could fill.

Our son's presence was crucial to me during those months. Just eleven, he was able to give me strength and support without which I would have completely retreated from life. I had not fully appreciated Dave's importance to me as a presence until that presence was no longer there. Because of our son, I was able to write and continue to fulfill my responsibilities. At the same time, I worked with my grief, crying often and little by little letting go of it.

Unlike the anguish of depression, which is corrosive, the pain of grief served a useful purpose. Underneath the loss and the stark necessity of living through every day without Dave was a sense of growth. For the first time in my life, I had to be both independent and responsible. The economic legacy was slight, and I had to devise a way of earning a living. I also had to make major decisions, such as whether or not to sell the house, where to send our son to school, and how to manage our budget. Although these were decisions I would have had to make even if Dave had lived, there was a profound difference in making them alone.

Dave had been a member of a funeral society which provided for simple cremation of his body and scattering of the ashes at sea. Of course we respected his wishes in the matter, and I felt no desire for a memorial service of any kind. However, in time I came to wish he had a grave, somewhere I could go to be near him, some spot to which to carry my grief. It was an oddly unexpected feeling. Without a grave for my flowers and my tears, I tended to identify his presence with the house in which we had lived for the last eleven years of his life and which contained all his books, papers, and pictures. Consequently, every time my son and I went anywhere, leaving the house was a terrible wrench. It was almost as if he were still living in the house and unable to care for himself.

This "grief work" went on, with greater or less intensity, during the first year following his death. In addition to the major loss of his presence, there were innumerable small losses: memories, dreams, hopes, that had to be faced. At times I grew very impatient with myself for still feeling grief after six or eight or ten months, for I did not want to become one of those eternally grieving widows. Now I know that it was necessary to let the grief take its course, much as an illness or a love affair must be allowed to progress. I tried to concentrate on all the good things we had shared, the immense happiness of our first years together, our joy in our first and only child. I wanted to put aside the old and dying Dave; but I found I could not—he was as much a part of our life together as the earlier, vivacious personality. If I were to give any advice to someone suffering the loss of a loved one, I would say it is most important not to try to avoid grief, but to express it as necessary, to live through it.

Finally, at the end of that first year, as I was standing in the kitchen making bread, I was overcome by a recognition of his absence that was more profound than any I had known before. He was gone, ever-gone, and I would know his living presence no more. It struck me with full force as an inescapable truth. I stood very still, enclosed in the feeling, and let go at last of the living/dying Dave. After that, I was able to write the following description of his death:

". . . At about 3:00 I was standing beside your bed when you stopped breathing. Just stopped. I was alarmed. Was this the end? Was this all there was? Then you started again, but it was different —long, labored, sighing breaths that you seemed to take reluctantly, almost as if you were forced to.

"I realized that this was the change Matyana Grogan of the Visiting Nurse Association had told me to expect and I called the VNA. As it happened she was there and we talked. She said she would call the doctor and did I have someone with me? I said I intended calling the Vedanta nuns next, which I did. Within 15 minutes, the head nun and another (a former practical nurse) were here. The head nun had brought some Ganges water and she sprinkled it on you, saying a little prayer. I wondered what you would think of that if you were aware enough to know it.

"But you never opened your eyes again and we stayed with you for the next two hours. Now and then you would stop breathing and then start again, always with that same air of unwillingness, as if you weren't quite ready yet. Each time you stopped breathing, it was as if you were letting go a little more, going one step farther away. It was all very peaceful and almost contented as if, now that the time had come, you welcomed it and wanted to cooperate. . . .

"At a little after 5:00 you stopped breathing for the last time. We felt for your pulse and could find none. You were very still and I leaned over and kissed your forehead. You were gone.

"It was a beautiful death, darling. Inspiring in the courage and serenity you showed. You let go little by little, taking each step as it came and I remembered the morning you told me how hard you had tried to die during the night. You died as you lived, meeting it directly and not asking or giving any quarter . . .

"I had managed to reach my sister by phone at 4:00 and she came in on the 8:25 flight. The nuns took me to the airport and when my sister came, I put my arms around her, buried my head in her shoulder and said, 'He's gone.' But I didn't cry. I was filled with the beauty of your death.

"Our son had been away all day but he came at about 11:00. Then there were three of us again, and my sister answered the phone all week-end while I stayed in bed, utterly exhausted.

"I still miss you. I shall always miss you. We had so much that was beautiful together and in my memory you will always be that brave, vital person I knew and loved."

Between the writing of this book and the present moment I have passed the half-century mark. (In fact, I gave myself a big birthday party to mark the accomplishment.) That is not old in today's society, yet it is a significant step toward aging. My hair is gray, my neck is wrinkled, I haven't the energy or the memory I once had. I still look forward to certain things I want to do and have to do, but there is something missing. I no longer believe that I am a special person, except in the sense that everyone is special.

When I look back on my youth, I sometimes wonder what connection there is between that naive and hopeful girl and the woman I have become. In my teens, I was regarded as a talented musician; I was gifted academically; I wrote well. Those early promises now seem meaningless. They had—and have—nothing to do with the significance of my life. They were exterior and unimportant.

What is important is that I try to live each day as it comes, giving, receiving, sharing to the best of my ability. Buddhist philosophy says that the path is the goal, and I am more and more convinced this is true. What I set out to achieve is not nearly so important as the way in which I work toward that achievement, whether it is making a loaf of bread or writing a book or meditating on the infinite. When the hand is played and the die is cast, it is the present moment—and only the present moment—that matters. What I do and say and think right now dictate what will happen tomorrow.

For this reason, it is important to me to spend a little time each day in meditation. Sometimes I pray, but I am not able to describe to whom or to what I pray. It is the quiet, interior moment that restores my sanity.

My illness made me selfish and liable to panic at the first sign of its recurrence. Thus, when I feel myself going down, I cry out for a stop and a look around at what is happening both inside and out. Often (usually?) I can do little or nothing about the exterior events, and there are times, too, when my inner life seems beyond my control. But if I can catch up and hold on for even a few minutes, it helps. It is a matter of exploring, of being ready and willing to take that quiet, interior momentary glimpse at myself.

I call this my spiritual life. That interior glimpse gives me continuity. Ultimately, I am neither the body nor the mind, but the spirit. This is where the meaning of my life lies, although I am unable to translate it into words. I still believe, as I did when I originally wrote this book, that no single answer is suitable for everyone. Each of us must find his or her own path, which means that each goal is unique. In that sense, I—and everyone—am special.

This book is about pain and the recovery from pain. It does not pretend to point to any panaceas. What is good for me may be meaningless for someone else. I can look at my life from many different aspects and each one gives me a different value for that life. I can look at myself and find many different people there, for I play whatever role is necessary or desirable or inevitable at the time. What, then, am I really? What are you?

For each of us the answer is different, and also it is the same. The spark of life which gives spiritual depth to my living is the same as the one which informs yours. How we go about finding it is what is different, and it is the "how" which carries us from moment to moment, from here to there. In this light, this book may be important as a study of the nature of mental illness and the processes of suicidal thinking; it may say things that have not been said in other sources. It is only one person's experience, but it speaks to and for many others who have been through similar trials or who wish to understand them.

PS
3569
.A828
Z463
1979